RELICS
and
MIRACLES

RELICS
and
MIRACLES
• •

TWO THEOLOGICAL ESSAYS

by

Sergius Bulgakov

Translated by

Boris Jakim

William B. Eerdmans Publishing Company

Grand Rapids, Michigan / Cambridge, U.K.

"On Holy Relics," written 1918, was originally published posthumously in a private edition
as *O sviatykh moshchiakh*, Paris, 1992.
"On the Gospel Miracles" was originally published privately as
O chudesakh evangel'skikh, Paris, 1932.

This English edition published 2011 by
Wm. B. Eerdmans Publishing Co.
2140 Oak Industrial Drive N.E., Grand Rapids, Michigan 49505 /
P.O. Box 163, Cambridge CB3 9PU U.K.

Printed in the United States of America

17 16 15 14 13 12 11   7 6 5 4 3 2 1

Library of Congress Cataloging-in-Publication Data

Bulgakov, Sergei Nikolaevich, 1871-1944.
[On holy relics. English]
Relics and miracles: two theological essays /
by Sergius Bulgakov; translated by Boris Jakim.
p.   cm.
ISBN 978-0-8028-6531-1 (pbk.: alk. paper)
1. Jesus Christ — Miracles. 2. Theology, Doctrinal. 3. Christianity —
Essence, genius, nature. 4. Relics. 5. Russkaia pravoslavnaia tserkov? — Doctrines.
I. Jakim, Boris.   II. Bulgakov, Sergei Nikolaevich, 1871-1944. O chudesakh
evangel'skikh. English.   III. Title.   IV. Title: On the Gospel miracles.

BT366.3.B8513   2011

235'.2 — dc23

2011016839

www.eerdmans.com

Contents

Translator's Introduction

1

Sergius Bulgakov wrote "On Holy Relics" (1918) and "On the Gospel Miracles" (1932) during a period of amazing theological productivity which began with *The Unfading Light* (1917) and lasted almost until his death in 1944. This period is dominated by the two trilogies, "Little" and "Great,"[1] the Little Trilogy comprising works on John the Baptist, the Mother of God, and angels; the Great Trilogy comprising works on Christ, the Holy Spirit, and the Church. One of the distinguishing features of these two trilogies is a mixture of systematic theology (Christology, pneumatology, ecclesiology) and devotional theology. During this period Bulgakov also wrote numerous shorter works,[2] which also exhibit such a mixture. "On Holy Relics" can be grouped with such works of sacramental theology as "The Holy

---

1. The Little Trilogy comprises *The Friend of the Bridegroom, The Burning Bush,* and *Jacob's Ladder.* The Great Trilogy comprises *The Lamb of God, The Comforter,* and *The Bride of the Lamb.*

2. Here is a grouping by category of the most important shorter works: Systematic theology: "The Icon and Its Veneration," "On the Gospel Miracles," "Hypostasis and Hypostatizedness," "Judas Iscariot: The Traitor-Apostle," "Chapters on Trinity." Sacramental theology: "On Holy Relics," "The Eucharistic Dogma," "The Holy Grail," "The Eucharistic Sacrifice," "Hierarchy and the Sacraments." Sermons: "Churchly Joy." Sophiology: "The Wisdom of God."

Grail," "The Eucharistic Dogma," and "The Eucharistic Sacrifice" (in fact, as we shall see, Bulgakov sees an intimate connection between the veneration of relics and the sacrament of the Eucharist). "On the Gospel Miracles," which Bulgakov calls a work of Christology, can be grouped with such shorter works of systematic theology as "The Icon and Its Veneration" and with such longer works as *The Friend of the Bridegroom* and *The Burning Bush*. It should be noted that the shorter works often serve as the "building blocks" forming the longer theological works; for example, "On the Resurrection of Christ," the final chapter of "On the Gospel Miracles," can be seen as the first iteration of the theology of the Resurrection developed in Bulgakov's magisterial work on Christology, *The Lamb of God*.

All of Bulgakov's theological works have a mystical element. All of them are to some extent examples of mystical theology, but this mystical element is usually more concentrated in the shorter works — the shortness seems to lend itself to greater intensity. This certainly holds true for both "On Holy Relics" and "On the Gospel Miracles." These two works remind us that Bulgakov is more than just a great theologian; he is also a mystic of the highest order. But what am I saying? All great theologians are also great mystics.

2

The occasion for the writing of "On Holy Relics" is the desecration of the relics of Russian saints by Bolshevik officials immediately after the Revolution. The desecration usually took the form of un-entombing the relics and of taking them apart with one's hands ("analyzing" them) until they were supposedly exposed to be nothing more than dust. Bulgakov writes the essay against such desecration, but what he really elaborates is a theology of relics. In fact, he is perhaps the first to attempt to develop a comprehensive theology of relics, connecting them with the Incarnation and showing their place in sacramental theology in general. He examines the status of the dogma of relics and points out that this dogma had not received a doctrinal definition at any of the ecumenical councils. It has not been the object of any special deliberation, but, like many important dogmas of the

Church, it has been accepted through the Church's practice. "It is simply that the veneration of holy relics became universal from the very beginning of the Church's existence, so natural was this veneration, responding to the direct emotion of the believer's heart" (p. 3 in the present volume).

Bulgakov avers that the veneration of holy relics is most intimately connected with the fundamental dogma of Christianity: with divine Incarnation for the sake of our salvation. Thus, the deification of man is the basis of the veneration of the saints, as well as of their bodily remains, holy relics (pp. 7-8). This ontological essence of man is the basis of what Bulgakov called "religious materialism." What this means is that, in the sacramental life of the Church, all spiritual things are also corporeal; all divine things have flesh, are human, for man is deified bodily. In other words, in the sacramental life of the Church, all spiritual things are clothed in matter, in a body, in flesh. Therefore, we perform all the sacraments having at our disposal a certain material of the sacrament — bread and wine, oil, myrrh, water, and, in the extreme case, word and touch. Therefore, we "sanctify" or "bless" water, icons, temples, and so on; and that, in general, is why we have holy things, holy places and objects. And that is also why we venerate holy relics. The distinctive character of holy relics can be understood by referring to the Holy Gifts of the Eucharist. In these Gifts we have the Most Precious Body and Blood of Christ in the form of bread and wine, substances of this world. For the sacrament of the Holy Eucharist it is essential that these be genuine bread and wine, which constitute the physical matter of the Holy Eucharist. Bulgakov points out that the bread and wine in the Holy Eucharist are analogous to the remains of a body in relation to its relics (see p. 32).

Bulgakov also points out the profound and intimate connection between the power of relics and the Lord's three-day sojourn in the grave: "Sanctifying with Himself all things, the Lord also sanctified the state of holy relics by the fact that His Most Pure Body abided in the grave for three days and three nights in the state of a holy relic, even though It later passed from this state into the state of total resurrection and transfiguration" (p. 23). "During the three-day sojourn in the grave the Lord's body too was in the state of a holy relic; in general, it was the archetype of holy relics" (p. 103). Like the Body of the Lord, the Body of the Mother of God too was taken up into heaven, rose from the dead, and was glorified, which is why one cannot speak of relics with regard to the Holy Body of the Mother of God, although it did pass through the state of holy relics during the three days of abiding in the grave. For Bulgakov this signifies a point of reference for that which corresponds to the nature of holy relics in the deification of the world: "This is the state of death in which, however, death has no power: Triumphant on the surface of phenomena, death is powerless in the essence of things; and this powerlessness of death, or the life of the deceased, is precisely the state of holy relics" (p. 24).

3

Bulgakov calls his essay "On the Gospel Miracles" a "chapter from Christology" (present volume, Author's Preface), and tells us that it can be fully understood only in connection with an integral Christological teaching. He further tells us that his essay considers one of the most acute questions of the Christian consciousness in the present age: the question of *human* activity in relation to the works of Christ. This question is motivated by the fact that, in Christ's divine-humanity, the whole fullness of the divine nature was united with the whole fullness of the human nature.

For Bulgakov, miracles are just as cosmic and law-governed as all natural phenomena: In relation to the cosmos, miracle must be judged to be natural, not supernatural and especially not unnatural. In other words, miracle refers not to the creation but to God's Providence for the world. But God as Providence acts in the world not by coercing it, but by guiding, through spiritual causality, the world's natural, or mechanical, causality. "This *union* of spiritual causality (through freedom) and mechanical, causality (through necessity) is what constitutes the character of the law governing the cosmos" (p. 52). For Bulgakov it is this spiritual-natural structure of the world that constitutes the permanent miracle of the world, the miracle of miracles as the foundation of all that is miraculous.

The character of spiritual power in the world can vary, for the freedom of creaturely spirits is capable of being directed either upward or downward, either toward God or toward the world, either from God or against God, both in the angelic and in the human world. From this come two inspirations, dark and light, and two orders of miracle, good and evil, or true and false. . . . The distinction between true and false miracles consists in the fact that true miracles are manifestations of the spiritual mastery of the world through spiritual causality according to God's will, and lead, in the final analysis, to the deification of the world through the communion of the latter with the God-Man by the power of Christ; whereas false miracles signify the appearance of human power in the world without the mastery of it with God's help. (pp. 52-53)

Bulgakov tells us that Christ's miracles are really signs of God's love for man: "In their content miracles are works of love and mercy; in their significance they are manifestations of human power in the world, human power that is reinforced and illuminated by God's power" (p. 78). Miracles such as the healing of spiritual and physical sicknesses in man, including the healing of death, are *human* tasks; they are *human* works of mercy and compassion; and, according to Bulgakov, all of them are tasks assigned to man as a natural being, who is placed by God as the lord of creation and endowed with the gift of compassionate love for man and for all creatures.

Man is destined to conquer or master the world through spiritual causality. In relation to the world man is a multipersonal cosmourge, a "master," conquering nature and subordinating it to his human purposiveness. This relation is implanted in man, and it must be understood religiously. Bulgakov distinguishes two pathways of causality: personal miracle-working and the cosmourgic conquest of nature. Human cosmourgy can mean different things:

first, humankind can be a cosmourge, like the Church, in the name of Christ, performing works of love and philanthropy, and then cosmourgy becomes a Christian miracle-working, not personal, but communal, ecclesial; and then the ecclesialization of the world occurs through cosmourgy. Secondly, humankind can make its cosmourgic power into an instrument that serves its natural essence damaged by sin, i.e., into an instrument that serves passions and the void. Thirdly and finally, cosmourgy can also become a pathway of theomachy, a satanical antagonism toward God and an exhibition of signs of *human* power, where man considers himself to be god. (p. 93)

Bulgakov affirms that all miracles, all human works, are subordinated to one great common work — the Resurrection of Christ: "The Resurrection of Christ is an ontological miracle which *takes us beyond* the limits of this world, even though it is accomplished in the latter; it is super-cosmic in the cosmos" (p. 95). The Resurrection is the Miracle of Miracles:

just as works have their integral in the Work, so miracles have their integral in the Miracle. . . . Man cannot know in advance what humankind will attain or not attain on its path. . . . The only thing we know is what man's goal is. The works of humankind serve life, which is God's abiding miracle in this world; and thus these works must lead this temporary life to the life of the resurrection, which is God's Work performed upon human works. The universal resurrection is therefore the divinely actualized integral of all of human history and all human works. (p. 113)

On Holy Relics
(In Response to Their Desecration)

In its God-hating cynicism and blasphemy, the desecration of holy relics that recently took place in Russia[1] does not have any precedents in the history of Christianity. The fury of the God-haters and the spirit of the Antichrist are fully evident in this savage profanation. Nevertheless, this is destined to be, and the heart of the believer must not tremble before this approaching abomination of desolation in the place of holiness. One is rather amazed by the inertia and restraint of the satanical gangsters in the Kremlin, which enjoys unlimited power and does not shy away from any means to achieve its goals. Evidently, the time has not yet come for the powers in the Kremlin to reveal the full magnitude of their hatred of Christianity, a hatred that constitutes the chief — and even unique — religious engine of the whole movement which is advancing under the banner of democracy and socialism and which, for now, has received its most

1. In the first years after the Revolution, Bolshevik officials tried to demonstrate that holy relics were a "deception" by uncovering the remains, taking them apart, and showing that usually there was nothing there but bones and dust. This is the desecration and "analysis" that Bulgakov is referring to. In the second paragraph of the present essay, we get an idea of the desecration that ensued from this "analysis": "There, where, in their pious humility, believers did not dare raise their eyes, and where a holy darkness reigned, electric lights were insolently brought in and filthy paws began to take apart the contents of the holy raka." — Translator.

decisive expression in Russian Bolshevism. But such a satanical assault against the believing heart as the analysis of holy relics requires, of course, an internal opposition from us. And for those who do not doubt that the Lord is leading and protecting His Church, it is clear that such assaults are also lessons being taught to us and questions that demand our answer. By its desecration of holy relics, a desecration that unquestionably has troubled many hearts, the satanical gangsters intended to destroy the faith in these relics; and since, in the life of the Church, all things are connected and it is impossible to remove a single little stone without shaking the whole edifice, it follows that the intentions of the Kremlin gangsters go even further: They are directed against the faith in the Church in general.

There, where, in their pious humility, believers did not dare raise their eyes, and where a holy darkness reigned, electric lights were insolently brought in and filthy paws began to take apart the contents of the holy raka.[2] By itself, this spectacle alone would have been sufficient to stagger and horrify us. However, many also felt surprise and disappointment: There, where one thought to find an incorruptible body, one found only parts of a body or even bones with clear signs of damage from the passage of time. The belief that one would find an incorruptible body was sustained in many by the naïvely pious custom of imparting to the remains of saints the form of an integral body, wrapped and rewrapped; it was difficult to discern that this supposed human figure was actually filled with wadding and, in general, was made by human hands. That which, of course, was not a deception, but only a pious custom (although perhaps an erroneous one), was interpreted as a deception and became an object of mockery. Meanwhile, without any answer stood people of faith, who had to choose between denial of a fact (of course, the sons of falsehood lied here as much as they lie always and everywhere, but not everything can be considered a lie) or denial of the holy relics — and it is the latter that the servants of the Antichrist tried to achieve. These servants created beforehand an atmosphere of mockery and profanation, for

---

2. A raised tomb containing the relics. It is usually placed in a church in such a way as to make the relics convenient for the veneration of the faithful. — Translator.

only in such an atmosphere is it possible to undertake something like the analysis of relics.

Can anyone conceive, without trembling, of digging up the grave of one's father, mother, or other relatives, of disturbing the repose of the grave in order to analyze what is contained there? And can a believing soul conceive such an idea in relation to a raka containing holy relics? A believing soul could not even think of such a thing, let alone carry out such an analysis. Therefore, holy relics have always remained inviolate; they can only be approached at definite times by pious servants of the Church, for the purpose of wrapping them or, in general, for some sacred action. But here a triumphant lout has approached the raka and, standing before it with hands on his hips in a pose of insolent challenge, he has turned everything inside out and declared that there is nothing there except dust and bones. We did not want to look, and did not look, but now we are compelled to look. There, where a holy ignorance once enveloped everything, the light of day is now installed; and we must ask questions of ourselves and provide answers. Such an analysis of relics has been permitted by Providence: we cannot doubt this. Here, as in other questions, one cannot allow one's intelligence to remain infantile; one must gain knowledge and understanding.

Thus, leaving disbelievers to celebrate their imaginary victory of insolence and spite, we, believers, must pose anew the following questions: What exactly are holy relics and what are the content and meaning of the dogma of the veneration of holy relics?

It is necessary to point out that this dogma had not received a doctrinal definition at any of the ecumenical councils. It has not been the object of any special deliberation, but, like many important dogmas of the Church, it has been accepted through the Church's practice. It is simply that the veneration of holy relics became universal from the very beginning of the Church's existence, so natural was this veneration, responding to the direct emotion of the believer's heart. And the struggle to preserve holy relics from desecration and destruction began very early, since even then pagans and the synagogue sought to destroy relics, while Christians preserved and venerated them. The rule according to which the liturgy is celebrated upon holy relics, sewn for this purpose into the antimension,[3] and according to which the holy altar has holy relics at its foundation, this rule became a part of the Church's practice early on and was confirmed by the Seventh Ecumenical Council.

At that time it was the remains of saints, and primarily of martyrs, that were considered to be holy relics; and of course no one considered them to be incorruptible in the sense of the complete preservation of the whole body, since parts of these remains had to be rescued from fire, from water, from amphitheaters. Furthermore, it was customary to divide these remains and to distribute their parts, with each part evidently being considered as an entire relic, i.e., as representing the entire body, in the same way that every particle of the Holy Eucharistic Gifts contains the Body and Blood of Christ. Clearly, this custom does not originate in the notion of the incorruptibility of holy relics in the sense of their physical indestructibility. In general, the attribute of *incorruptibility*, which has been advanced to the foreground in modern times, was not emphasized then: At most, one spoke then only of the incorruptibility of *certain* relics, since this attribute was clearly inapplicable to their most important and broadest category, that of the holy martyrs. The *holiness*, not the incorruptibility, of holy relics was at the center of how people understood them.

We are not able to say exactly when and how the attribute of physical incorruptibility advanced to the forefront and occupied such an inappropriate place. In Russia, this was due to the combined result of inferior seminary theologizing and official hypocrisy, which intentionally obscured the actual state of things and reinforced a too easy belief that could just as easily become disbelief. In the people's view, all holy relics were venerated as incorruptible bodies; and, perhaps in an effort to conform to this veneration, holy relics were intentionally given the form of an integral body even when such a body did not exist. Of course, there have existed (and exist) such cases where holy relics remain incorruptible by God's will. However,

---

3. The antimension (from the Greek: "instead of the table") is among the most important furnishings of the altar in Orthodox Christian liturgical traditions. It is a rectangular piece of cloth, of either linen or silk, typically decorated with representations of the entombment of Christ, the four Evangelists, and scriptural passages related to the Eucharist. A small relic of a saint is sewn into it. — Translator.

if the essence of holy relics consisted in physical incorruptibility, we would then have to consider as relics not only Egyptian mummies but also bodies preserved in the ground as a result of particular soil conditions (so-called natural mummification); and one would also have to recognize that certain remains of great saints, universally venerated by the whole Church, are not holy relics. The glorification of the relics of St. Seraphim represented such a case that led some minds astray:[4] At first there was official silence about the contents of his tomb; and then, when the enemies of the Church gained information about this and publicized it (of course, with their own interpretation), the ecclesiastical authorities had to provide an explanation. Referring to the authority of Professor Golubinsky (instead of to the incontrovertible authority — ecclesial tradition and the ecclesial consciousness), the ecclesiastical authorities began to assert that incorruptibility does not constitute an essential attribute of holy relics. Strictly speaking, the question that life imperatively poses before us now was already posed then, but then it fell victim to an inappropriate ecclesiastical morality and to a censorship which, of course, did not serve the Church, because doubt, unconscious and driven inward, continued to do its destructive work, something that has come to the surface today. Likewise, when the relics of St. Germogen were uncovered, this question was left in shadow.

4. In 1903, Seraphim of Sarov was glorified as a saint by the Russian Orthodox Church. As part of this process, on July 3, 1903, the saint's relics were moved from their original burial place to the church of Saints Zosimus and Sabbatius, where they remained until the day of the glorification. On July 18, at the time of the Litia during Vespers, the saint's coffin was carried from the church of Saints Zosimus and Sabbatius and into the Dormition Cathedral at Sarov. During Matins, as the Polyeleos "Praise ye the Name of the Lord . . ." was sung, the coffin was opened. After the Matins Gospel, Metropolitan Anthony and the other hierarchs venerated the relics. They were followed by the royal family, the officiating clergy, and all the people into the cathedral. On July 19, the saint's birthday, the late Liturgy began at eight o'clock. At the Little Entrance, twelve Archimandrites lifted the coffin from the middle of the church, carried it around the altar, then placed it into a special shrine that had been constructed for them. Bulgakov implies that, when Seraphim's relics were uncovered, the church authorities were silent about their condition, which led to rumors that they had decomposed and were thus not physically incorruptible. The church authorities, basing their argument on the scholarship of the church historian E. Golubinsky, asserted that physical incorruptibility is not an essential attribute of holy relics. — Translator.

There is no debate that, among wide circles of the people, as well as among enemies of the Church (at least those who are sincere and do not lie), there is agreement that incorruptibility, i.e., preservation of the entire body from decomposition, is an essential attribute of relics. However, it has never seemed possible to apply this attribute to all relics, since there have always been saints whose relics either have not been preserved at all, or whose relics have been preserved only in parts, and sometimes only in very small parts indeed; but this has in no wise diminished the veneration of these saints. Furthermore, even the bodies of saints that have been preserved incorruptibly have sometimes been subject to partial decomposition; and here, evidently, quantitative distinction does not have any significance. It is sufficient for corruptibility to appear in a single finger for the entire attribute of incorruptibility to be voided. Finally, there have been cases where remains that showed no traces of incorruptibility were venerated as holy relics. Thus, "incorruptibility," understood as the absence of obvious signs of decomposition, could be either present or absent. We admit that this attribute is most natural and proper to the bodies of saints, so that the opposite case represents an anomaly that requires special explanation; nevertheless, it is clear that the essence of holy relics does not consist in their incorruptibility; the latter constitutes only a derivative attribute.

In general, one must reject the notion that holy relics have inalienable *physical* attributes; such do not exist. Usually, in the act of the glorification of a saint (canonization), the reasons for the glorification are enumerated. First among these is incorruptibility, followed by verified miracles such as (medically unexplainable) healings and other suchlike miracles of the *physical* order. Even without mentioning the fact that such physical miracles cannot be indisputable and, moreover, always have an *asylum ignorantiae*,[5] i.e., a possible explanation on the basis of natural laws that are as yet unknown; even without mentioning this, it is clear that both miracles and incorruptibility are only *reasons* for the glorification, not its cause; the cause wholly and uniquely consists in the holiness and Spirit-bearingness of the

---

5. Refuge of ignorance, an explanation that one finds satisfactory in order to avoid further thought. — Translator.

glorified saint. When I was at the Council[6] I asked one of the notable Russian bishops who had participated in the glorification of a great Russian saint, whether our Church has any rules regarding the glorification of saints corresponding to the "process" in Catholicism, and he answered that it does not: The Holy Spirit guides the Church in such cases. This answer might appear to be unsatisfying, but it is the only possible and rational one. At least, there cannot be, and must not be, any other answer. All "reasons" are only occasions for the crystallization of the ecclesial consciousness, which, strictly speaking, does not even require them; and it is necessary to separate in advance the physical characteristics of relics from their essence. Thus, there arises before us in all its breadth the fundamental problem of the veneration of holy relics.

What constitutes the meaning of the dogma of relics, and what are holy relics? It is likely that, in a certain portion of our Church community (and possibly even among the clergy), there exists a skeptical and indifferent attitude toward this question. These members of the community would prefer to be as silent as possible regarding this question in order to avoid extraneous scandals: The veneration of holy relics is thought to be an unnecessary superstition, which can be, and in essence must be, avoided. The entire weight of historical slanders against the veneration of holy relics, together with our contemporary blasphemous attitude, presses on the frail consciousness of such members of the Church community and inclines this consciousness to take the broad path — to divest itself of superfluous and unnecessary doctrines and of the practice corresponding to them. Of course, it is difficult to pre-decide what sort of divestment is desired: Perhaps there is a readiness here to divest all sacraments from the Church and to leave nothing except a Protestant service of the word. But those who in fact do not desire to go so far, but only wish to eliminate the veneration of holy relics, must take clear account of the fact that all things are connected organically in the Church teaching, and that it is impossible to remove a single part of it. And, in particular, the veneration of holy relics is most intimately connected with the fundamental dogma of Christianity — with divine Incarnation for the sake of our salva-

6. Presumably, the All-Russian Church Council of 1917-1918. — Translator.

tion. The *deification of man, Christian human-divinity* (if it is permissible to use this phrase), is the basis of the veneration of the saints, as well as of their bodily remains, holy relics.

God became man in order that man become God: God's humanization has as a direct consequence the deification of man, gives to man an ontological foundation. Between heaven and earth, between God and man, an eternal ladder was erected after Christ went both downward and upward with His flesh as, with Him, did His Most Pure Mother. After the descent of the Holy Spirit, grace ceaselessly flows into the world, and the world becomes a receptacle of divine powers. This outpouring of powers is accomplished by means of holiness, which itself is produced by this outpouring; in the divine liturgy, in sacraments, it nourishes, warms, and preserves the world and man. All sacraments in the strict sense, and also all holy acts that are usually not called sacraments, represent a ceaseless bringing-down of this power into man. All and sundry immediately tell us that this is a spiritual power, and that one can and must speak only of birth in the Spirit, of service in the Spirit. This word and notion "spiritual" has been endlessly abused in all epochs (and perhaps it has been abused most eagerly by those who do not believe in the existence of any spiritual principle in man). One must state this simply, directly, and briefly: Although an eternal, immortal, and divine spirit lives in man, man himself is by no means a spiritual (i.e., only a spiritual) being; he also has a body and is therefore a spiritual-bodily being. Man is not an angel; rather, he is man, a cosmic being, a cosmos, an anthropocosmos; and nothing cosmic is alien to him or (one must emphasize) can or should be alienated from him.

How can one understand this inseparability of the spiritual and the cosmic, this mystery of the creation of man? There is perhaps no answer to this. That is how things are. And the human spirit does not know any life except human, i.e., cosmic, life. In man and through man circulate constantly and continuously all the powers of the universe, of which he is the center; in him, for him, and through him, the world is created, and all of his actions are not only spiritual movements, but also cosmic actions. He is capable of turning to God from the world, but God, who created him, does not take him out of the world, but only fills him with His power. This ontological essence of man contains the reason why, in the divine liturgy, in the mysterious side of the Church, there is manifested that which is called — at times with censure, and at times defiantly — religious materialism.

Although the life of the Church, which is concentrated in sacramental acts, always involves spiritual life, it never separates in man the spirit from his human essence. There is no sacrament of spirit, although all sacraments have a spiritual nature and are accomplished in the spirit, and this is the case simply because man is man, not a spirit. And this is most directly, clearly, and essentially expressed in the sacrament of Holy Eucharist, where the Lord gives Himself in His Body and Blood. The spiritual bread, the heavenly food, is also bodily bread and food; by no means does the spiritual sacrament become incorporeal — rather, it is corporeal to the highest degree, corporeal par excellence. So many disputes and misinterpretations were provoked by the Eucharistic debates, in which there was a lack of will to fully accept and understand man's ontological essence, the fact that he is not a spiritual being but a spiritual-corporeal being, the fact of his anthropocosmicity, which is why everything that involves man and, first and foremost, the divine food offered to him, the Holy Eucharist, must also have such a nature, must be theo-anthropocosmic, never breaking the ontological bond by which man is united with the world — for, to break this bond, to introduce spiritual, anticosmic sacrament, would be to destroy man and the world with him. But, as the Lord says about Himself, He came not to destroy the world but to save it. Therefore, in the gracious life of the Church, all that is spiritual is corporeal; all that is divine has flesh, is human, for man is man-god — all that is spiritual is material, is clothed in a body. Therefore, we perform all the sacraments having at our disposal a certain material of the sacrament — bread and wine, oil, myrrh, water, and, in the extreme case, word and touch. Therefore, we "sanctify" or "bless" water, icons, temples, and so on; and that, in general, is why we have holy things, holy places and objects. And that is also why we venerate holy relics.

To find suspect or to reject the veneration of holy relics on the basis of considerations of false spiritualism, i.e., to separate the relics from their possessors or bearers, is to reject both the humanity of the saints and one's own humanity. If the saints are holy, then their remains — their relics — are holy too; and these remains must be reverently preserved and venerated; in them and through them we address the glorified saints; by kissing them, we show our love for these saints. All that is human is not spiritual in the anticosmic sense; rather, it is cosmic, incarnate, has flesh, but this flesh is not dead matter, for it is permeated and sanctified by spirit, and that is why all sacraments, inasmuch as they are human, have, for man, matter and body — they are cosmic, they are human. That which is not cosmic, that which is abstract or negatively spiritual — is void, does not exist. And the opposite is also true: that which is only material, not spiritualized, lifeless — does not exist, is not human. In man, all that is material is alive, connected, unified.

Sacrament is the union of the human-cosmic with the divine-supramundane. God's power descends into the world and transforms it at definite moments and points, filling it with another life. Man is incapable of understanding how that which is creaturely and cosmic can be united with that which is self-sufficient and supracosmic; but this is what constitutes the power and mystery of sacrament. In the end, all particular questions concerning sacraments are reducible to a single, universal, and fundamental question — the question concerning the divine Incarnation of Christ the Savior: How is this Incarnation possible? For in Him, in Man, the whole fullness of divinity was made incarnate bodily. And sacraments are continuing and ceaselessly ongoing divine Incarnations; they represent the deification of the creature, a deification that was accomplished once in universal form at the descent of the Holy Spirit. This power is given to the Church by Christ and is ceaselessly sustained through holiness, which brings down the divine force. Sacrament transubstantiates the cosmic and makes it transcendent in relation to the world, in relation to itself; the nature of the cosmic becomes an incarnate antinomy, because, on the one hand, its "matter" is necessarily cosmic, belongs to this world (otherwise the sacrament would not be accomplished, for it must have an object, is accomplished in the world and above the world) and, on the other hand, it makes the matter transcendent in relation to itself.

It is by no means a question of some physical transformation of matter, i.e., a transformation within the limits of the cosmos and the states of matter. Any such transformation, however grandiose and destructive it might be, would be negligible in comparison with that internal catastrophe of being which takes place in sacrament, where the cosmic stops being itself and becomes supracosmic, divine. Therefore, both the occult[7] and even physical properties assumed (or not assumed) by the matter of the sacrament are derivative consequences of that which has taken place; furthermore, these properties can be present or absent, and are by no means commensurate with the change of the essence itself that has taken place. Holy water — according to liturgical books and to a large body of experiential evidence — does not grow stale; however, even if it sometimes does grow stale, it does not stop being itself. The prosphoron (the bread of the Eucharist) too can spoil at times, but it remains itself; and even the reserve Holy Gifts, the Body and Blood of Christ, can spoil at times, but they too remain themselves. Cosmic matter externally (but only externally) preserves its nature and power when another power and another essence are placed into it. Cosmic matter is permeated and transilluminated throughout the depths of its entire being; it acquires a nature other than itself, while its cosmic nature, as long as the cosmos stands, remains untouched: matter is so transparent and permeable for the divine power that it does not notice this power as it were, so that one space of being encompasses another, completely incompatible being, with the former not noticing the latter; and it is perfectly possible for disbelief to deny everything, for that which is taking place can be seen only with the eyes of belief. One of the Orthodox teaching guides says that if the Holy Gifts assume the visible form of the Body and Blood, one should put them aside and, instead, offer communion only in the form of the bread and wine concealed by the Holy Gifts.

The miracle of sacrament consists not in the transformation of matter, but in the total abolition of matter, while simultaneously preserving its natural properties. The power of sacrament in matter cannot be defined by any conceptual definition, even the most subtle one; in the eyes of science and of this world in general, the matter of sacrament is cosmic matter, fundamentally not different in all its properties from all other cosmic matter; and it is this inaccessibility of sacrament to measurement that

---

7. By "occult" properties Bulgakov means hidden or invisible spiritual properties. — Translator.

constitutes its property and its triumph. It is true that the objects of sacrament *can* have a palpable effect in the world; they can have properties that are perceived by sensitive natures; but nevertheless this refers to the periphery: Whatever the transformation of the "Body" of a given body might be, the internally fundamental transformation nevertheless remains beyond the limits of scientific investigation.

In sacrament, the transcendent enters into the immanent; heaven and earth are united in such a way that they stop existing in their separateness and oppositeness. This is accomplished wholly and uniquely by divine power, *by the grace of God.* It is accomplished through the sacrament of the Name of God: Invocation and sanctification by the Name of God bring down the power of God; transubstantiation takes place. All of the Church's sacramental and liturgical acts are only a sacrament of the Name; there operates here not a physical, i.e., cosmic, power, of whatever order, but a supracosmic, divine power, which acts both within and above the cosmos, transubstantiating it, while leaving its powers inviolate. Spiritual power and energy are implanted within a physical body.

One can express this idea in another way, in Kantian terms: A cosmic phenomenon is inhabited by a supracosmic noumenon; in sacrament, phenomenon stops corresponding to noumenon, and vice versa. The *action* of sacrament is exclusively spiritual, and it is cosmic only through the intermediary of spirit; and conversely: the power of the cosmos, of the "laws of nature," retains its power in phenomenal being. The "laws of nature" are not abolished when nature itself is abolished; that is what happens in sacrament. At the same time (and here is the other side of the antinomy of sacrament) the divine power that abolishes nature is indissolubly connected not only with nature in general but with a definite point of nature — with the matter of this sacrament. The chief defect of Kant's entire philosophy, a defect that is most salient in his religious philosophy and makes it a barren fig tree, consists in this opposition, which, in essence, is a separation. Without distinguishing nuances, Kant asserts, as do all of his followers, that that which is noumenal cannot be phenomenal, but rather is opposite to the phenomenal; and Kant finds the most powerful objections against the concreteness of religion in this opposition.

Meanwhile, from Kant's own doctrine, one could derive the opposite:

a *positive* doctrine of phenomenality as the sacrament of the noumenal, which has a depth, many depths, and through the phenomenal are visible the depths of the transcendent. Kant transformed the antinomy of the phenomenal and the noumenal, their conjugateness, into oppositeness and discontinuity, thereby transforming the world into a phantom and mask and the noumenal into an extracosmic, anticosmic power. In Kant was manifested the spiritual sickness of false spiritualism, which is so easily transformed into its double — materialism. More correctly, it is the case that this false spiritualism presupposes materialism, because there occurs in it an unnatural break between matter and spirit, asserting the polarity, the mutual impermeability and alienatedness, of matter and spirit, which is why materialism is natural and inevitable. By contrast, the Christian understanding (indeed, not only the Christian understanding, but the religious understanding in general, which has its practical realization in cult) affirms the continuity of the connection between the spiritual and the material, or the empirical and the noumenal. And this continuity objectively grounds the existence of *holy* things, of holy places, objects, and sacraments, all of which comes down to the recognition of spiritual flesh, of holy and glorified flesh, according to the teaching of the apostle Paul about the nature of the natural body and the spiritual body. And the sanctification of the flesh comes precisely from this continuity.

One can debate how best to philosophically develop this fundamental and primary fact of religious consciousness; but on the basis of prejudices of bad philosophizing, it is not permissible to separate — to the glory of meaningless materialism — spirit and flesh and to proclaim the world to be a dead machine. In fact, both for the most extreme materialism and for the most extreme spiritualism and idealism, there remains in force the problem of how consciousness is possible in man, a spiritual-material being; and one must affirm that neither materialists nor idealists are able to solve this problem. If one rejects the prejudice of Kantianism and materialism and sees in cosmic matter a living body, flesh that is potential and in the process of being actualized, then the idea of the sanctification of matter in sacrament and ritual and the significance of this sanctification as the unifier of the two worlds, the transcendent and the immanent, will turn out to be understandable, natural, logical, and self-evident. Spiritual acts and states are connected and implanted in things, and are transmitted by and through things — that is what we learn from the practice of the Christian cult, whose fundamental and unifying principle is the idea of *holy flesh*, of the spiritual body, of the unity and inseparability of flesh and spirit. And the natural and self-evident consequence of this is the religious materialism with which, from the time of Protestantism, it has been customary to reproach the practices of the Church, equating these practices with paganism, mystagogy, magic, sorcery, and fetishism.

Fetishism! That is the *ultima ratio* in the name of which the idea of religious cult is considered to be totally refuted in our day. In the face of such a profound error as materialism under the pretext of spiritualism, or vice versa, it is even necessary, without being frightened of our epoch, to come out in defense of fetishism, for the latter nonetheless contains a greater truth than abstract, i.e., materialistic, spiritualism. More precisely, it is necessary simply to state that fetishism is a truth, although one that is only a derivative, dialectical moment of the total truth, a moment taken outside of the general fundamental connectedness of the moments of the truth; and it is necessary to demonstrate the existence of this connectedness in order to remove the odium associated with fetishism and to reveal the very important truth contained in it, a truth that was evident to the natural, unobscured consciousness of the savage.

Fetishism is false, perhaps, not because it is the worship of sacred objects, fetishes, but only because the religious idea behind this worship is meager, false, imprecise, obscure. When a savage worships some stone, associating it with the presence of some lower or evil spirit, and the stone becomes a fetish, the falsity of this worship consists not in worship of the stone but in the worship of the spirit itself, which does not at all deserve worship, which is why here we can have, instead of a good and — *sit venia verbo*[8] — grace-bestowing fetishism, outright demonism or black magic. By contrast, when Jacob, after his sleep in the desert, poured oil upon the top of the pillar, and "called the name of that place Bethel" (the house of God) (Gen. 28:18-19), he accomplished an act of righteous, pious fetishism. God appeared to Jacob there, and he learned that that place was holy,

---

8. "May this word be forgiven." — Translator.

full of the presence of God. But, after all, God is not connected with a place. However, this was well understood even by those who connected His presence with a definite place; thus, Solomon, at the consecration of the Temple, clearly states that God does not live in a temple made by human hands, but that nevertheless there is a special presence of God in the Temple. This is what the power and mystery of concreteness, of the connection of the phenomenal with the noumenal, consist in. For God's omnipresence — more precisely, His presence outside all places, His extra-spatiality, His freedom from all limits of space and time — expresses His extramundane and supra-empirical essence; but this does not at all signify the general accessibility or ubiquity of His presence; it does not signify that He makes no distinction as to places. Inasmuch as the Absolute is God for the world and man, the Absolute takes upon itself the kenosis of empirical phenomenal being; God does not destroy but fulfills the foundations of creatureliness, spatiality, and temporality, which were called into being by Him Himself; and therefore He connected Himself with spatiality and temporality by a voluntary act of love and condescension, in order to come close to man: space and time exist for God too. This does not mean that space and time set a limit to His omnipotence, i.e., to His freedom; it does not mean that they are included in the absolute Essence of God; rather, it means that, insofar as God is present in the world and in man (more precisely, simply in man, for the world is Man, the anthropocosmos), He lives in space and time; and places and times are not a matter of indifference in this Being of God's. In other words, God is not present everywhere; and when He is present, He is present not by His omnipotence, but by His grace-bestowing power, and there are holy, God-chosen places as well as places forsaken by God. By the power of His divinity the Lord Jesus Christ could be present simultaneously in all spheres ("in the grave in the flesh,"[9] and so on), but as the God-Man He lived in the Holy Land and sanctified by His presence only certain definite places (all that has been said here about place holds also for holy times and seasons, but, in order not to lose the thread of our discussion, let us not stray too far from our subject).

9. From the Paschal Hours troparion. — Translator.

Therefore, fetishism too (i.e., the religious veneration of definite places and objects, i.e., religious concreteness) is fundamentally correct and justified. It is in this concreteness in general that we find the general foundation of cult, i.e., of practical divine veneration and divine liturgy. Outside of space and time, i.e., outside of holy places, acts, and objects, cult does not exist; and outside of cult, religion does not exist (the most we can have is religious philosophy). This "fetishism" can receive a special justification in Christianity, as the religion of divine Incarnation. In paganism fetishism was founded on the ineradicable but unclarified consciousness that the world is God's altar, that the world contains divinity; but this consciousness was clouded by an insufficient differentiation between the world and God, by a divinization of the world, which is totally opposite to the idea of the theosis of the world through the divine Incarnation. However, despite being clouded in this way, even in pagan fetishism this idea was not completely without truth; it is not eliminated in Christianity, but clarified and confirmed. Indeed, what is the Old Testament cult if not a gigantically overgrown fetishism, which is in fact what the enemies of religion call it in their infatuation with spiritualistic materialism? And we have this very same "fetishism" — but now totally purified, justified, and illuminated — in the Christian cult, and in particular in the veneration of holy places and of holy relics.

All considerations based on spiritualism and materialism must be rejected in advance, and we readily accept the accusation of fetishism, although we consider this to be not an accusation but rather the statement of a certain fundamental religious fact. To those who see fetishism in every *concreteness* of divine veneration, which in general characterizes cult, it must be stated directly that this fetishism is an inalienable trait of religious phenomenology without which there could be no religion, and that one should unhesitantly speak of holy places, holy objects, holy sacraments, and holy liturgical acts, even if rationalism stigmatizes all of this with the name of fetishism.

Of course, the Spirit of God lives in the Church, and all things in the Church are sanctified by His power and presence; all *holy* things (and in the Church all things are holy) are His action. However, we can distinguish different modes of this sanctification; in particular, in the question of holy relics, we can distinguish two fundamental modes of holiness — the mode of descent and the mode of ascent.

The Church is given the power of holiness and sanctification, and she applies and actualizes this power in all of her sanctifying and sacramental acts. The mode of this actualization is the invocation of the Holy Spirit — during the blessing of the Holy Gifts, during the blessing of water, during all blessings. The Church is given in priesthood this mysterious power to transubstantiate by the power of the Holy Spirit; and this, strictly speaking, is what sanctification is. There have been many disputes about words and about the very idea of transubstantiation apropos of the Eucharist, but the question has a general significance for every sanctification, which, in fact, is what transubstantiation is. That physical shell which is preserved with all of its properties no longer corresponds to what actually exists here, for what exists here is an object of another world, of the future age, of the transfigured earth; the physical reality here is only an appearance, an opaque veil behind which incorruptible holy flesh is found. This sanctification, and also transubstantiation, is an ontological catastrophe, a total discontinuity and nonconformity to law, which, thus, do not fit into Kant's schemes and are rejected by them. Sanctification cannot be understood *on the basis* of the nature of the creature and the particularity of a given object; this nature and this particularity do not present any inherent givens or foundations for sanctification, although there is here a mysterious conformity, a designation for some particular goal (e.g., even though bread and wine do not, of course, have any basis in themselves for transubstantiation into the Body and Blood, precisely they are designated for this goal, just as water is designated for blessing, and so on). Sanctification is accomplished not by the powers of the world but by supraphysical powers; this is a descending power, descending into the world from the extramundane, supramundane, divine sphere.

The mystery of sanctification, as well as the antinomy of the latter, an antinomy that inevitably confronts all gnosis,[10] however far it might go in removing the veils and shells of cosmic being, consists in this unification

10. By "gnosis," Bulgakov means human knowledge unaided by divine grace. — Translator.

or transubstantiation of the physical and supraphysical, of yes and no, of the world and the not-world, of God and not-God. But this is also the mystery of the *creation* of the world by God, a mystery that lies beyond the limits of the creaturely consciousness and leads into the supra-creaturely (thus, this mystery, hopelessly and forever transcending the limits of Kantian reason, can through grace be encompassed by the consciousness of one who, having developed this reason with its schemata, enters into a gracious, supra-creaturely state, for here too Christ's words are applicable: for men it is impossible, but for God it is possible). The abiding of the world in the extra-divinity proper to it and its deification by the descent of God into the world are two sides of one and the same antinomic act of world-creation: *The world is created on antinomy.* The Church is given the power of sanctification, which is divine power, the power of the Name of God. All liturgical activity, as well as all sacramental action, is the power of the Name of God given to the serving priests. *The Name is the ladder between earth and heaven;* by the Name are accomplished sanctification and sacramental action, which are only an extended form of the invocation of the Name. Here we do not propose to examine this question in detail; we shall limit ourselves to the affirmation that all sanctifications are mysterious actions of the Name, inscriptions of the sacred Tetragram. But the actions of this power are multifarious and concrete, and therefore the holy objects themselves are diverse. In particular, all cultic holy things, the temple, icons, and so on, are inscriptions of the Name. What is significant for the holiness of the icon is not the iconic image itself (for that would be only a picture or schema), but the sanctification by the Name, while the image is only a hieroglyph of the Name. The icon is a sacrament of the Name; this property of the icon remained undisclosed at the Seventh Ecumenical Council, where the veneration of icons was defined.

We find another kind of holiness in the mode of ascent; the *human* holiness of sainthood — and therefore the holiness of holy relics — belongs to this mode. Of course, human sainthood too is possible only on the pathway of grace; without grace, human powers would not be capable of becoming other than themselves, of being transubstantiated. The highest *human* virtue or quality, which is constantly being confused with sainthood, is not sainthood, has a different nature from sainthood. The human holiness that constitutes sainthood is of the same order as holiness in general; human sainthood is supramundane and thus suprahuman in its ontogeny, but it is human in its actualization. There are two poles of human-divinity: human self-deification to which are applicable St. Augustine's words that man without God is a diabolical being; and the gracious deification of man, helping him to become holy. Sainthood is human-divinity actualized by human exploit on the basis of God's grace. Outside of the divine incarnation and the action of God's grace, sainthood *in actu* is impossible, remaining an unattainable goal. By contrast, all Christians possess the calling to sainthood and the will to sainthood. And in saints this will attains actualization, i.e., the divine energies outweigh to such an extent the lower, sinful, human energies that a certain transubstantiation takes place in the very essence of man: He becomes a true superman — and thus a true man — with a nature different from his own.

A saint is one in whom there has already been accomplished the beginning of human transubstantiation, i.e., resurrection, prior to the universal resurrection, when by the will of God it will be accomplished for all — for some as resurrection to life, for others as resurrection to judgment. Here, this is the first resurrection.

In sainthood, man stops being man by making in himself a place for God; but thereby he becomes truly man. The path of sainthood is the crucifixion of the natural man, the removal from oneself of the natural man, self-renunciation, as well as, at the same time, the salvation, restoration, preservation of individuality. Only a saint has true individuality, integrated by integral wisdom,[11] and therefore he is a focus through which stream rays of grace. Sainthood is the rationally unfathomable mystery of the union of the Divine and the human, a mystery which in the God-Man was accomplished once for always in an absolute form, but which therefore can be accomplished in a man-God[12] too by the sanctifying power of grace, by human deification. Every sacrament — and especially Holy

11. Integral wisdom (Russian: *tselomudrie;* Greek: *sophrosyne*) is the spiritual wholeness of a man that makes him pure. The Russian word *tselomudrie* can also mean chastity. — Translator.

12. That is, the saint. — Translator.

Communion — yields such human deification, but in sainthood this union of the Divine and the human receives a stable and lasting character, so that man's nature is changed: "if any man be in Christ, he is a new creature" (2 Cor. 5:17).

It is necessary to distinguish sainthood as a divine state, or human deification, from human effort, energy, success: The human can become an altar for divine power — and then it is the human side of sainthood, but it can also turn out to be an altar for the human ego, and consequently for Luciferian pride. Therefore, sainthood exists only in the Church and is, in essence, actual ecclesialization, for the Church is holy (we do not take it upon ourselves here to define the inner and outer bounds of the Church, for the outer bounds might not coincide with the inner ones, and we would get the incommensurability that the Gospel speaks of so insistently, namely that the first will be last and the last will be first, and that many prophecies and miracles done in the Name of Christ will be rejected by Him as unknown to Him). In his person the saint manifests the act of divine-humanity, the accomplished victory of the deification of the creature. Therefore, the very state of sainthood, i.e., of God-bearingness or Spirit-bearingness, remains unknown to us sinners; we can only catch some of the rays of sainthood, observe some of the manifestations of the latter.

It is important to keep in mind that sainthood is not only sinlessness, but also has a *positive* significance: there is a radical difference between an infant whose sinlessness is most clearly manifested in the ecclesial consciousness in the ritual of infant burial, and sainthood as an attainment of maturity, as a victory over sinful human nature. The infant is called "blessed," not a "saint";[13] the infant's state, compared to that of the saint, is passive; it is characterized not by the presence of something positive but only by the absence of what is opposite to sainthood. The infant's nature is a sinful human nature that has not been overcome in the infant; it just has had no time to develop because of the interruption of life, which, of course, constitutes a providential mystery. The "new creature" also has

13. In Orthodoxy, the term "blessed" is considered to indicate a lower degree of holiness than the term "saint." — Translator.

a new nature: a special physics, physiology, psychology, which only a spiritual man can see and understand. Here, sainthood, like everything else in religion, is absolutely concrete and individual; it is an actualization of individuality, the acquisition of one's own person. The saint is an abiding point in the world that cosmic transubstantiation cannot touch, for this point is already transubstantiated, although the time of transfiguration, i.e., the time of the coming in glory, has not yet come: Glory is still shut off by flesh, just as it was shut off outside of transfiguration in the days of the Savior's earthly life, although it continued to abide in the world.

As we pointed out above, this concreteness and individuality necessarily extend to the body, or, more precisely, to the entire human pneumo-corporeal nature (for man's body does not exist separately from his spirit, just as fleshless human spirit does not exist). Saints are holy in both body and soul; holy in them is their body, which in this sense during their life as well as after death (which in this respect does not change anything) is a *relic*, i.e., a *place of the holy body*. In the rite of burial given in the Trebnik[14] the body is in general called a relic, perhaps as an indication of the fact that it can be a receptacle for a *holy* relic. Death does not have power over a holy body in the sense that that rupture which it usually causes between body and soul does not occur here. The saint retains power over and connection with his body, which, as spirit-bearing, becomes so spiritualized that it is not subordinate to death. "Repose in relics" signifies the preservation of the connection with the body and — to that extent — the overcoming of death, the coming into the future age: John 6:24. Precisely here we are confronted with a whole series of perplexing questions regarding the nature of holy relics, questions that have now become more acute because of the recent desecration of relics. The first of these questions is: If saints manifest in their person an overcoming of death as the rupture between soul and body, what, then, is their death? Is it only a swoon? No, it is indeed death, physically similar in all things — or almost in all things — to common death; the decomposition of holy relics is the best proof of this.

---

14. Literally, the Book of Needs, a collection of Orthodox prayers and rites. — Translator.

To fathom experientially or to understand rationally the mystery of death, that which takes place during the mysterious separation of the inseparable, is something that is impossible for us, despite all the theosophical guidebooks to the afterlife that are currently available. But the whole of Christian anthropology leaves no doubt that the most agonizing of ruptures takes place during this violent disincarnation, for death is ontologically unnatural. However, there can be substantial differences in this rupture, in this passage through the gates of death. Death entered through sin and is defeated by perfect sinlessness. The Lord tasted death, having abided for three days in the grave. Did His Most Pure Body undergo decomposition? To this terrible and even terrifying question we are given an answer by the teaching of the Church. It is true that the Lord assumed human flesh in all things and to the end. He was beaten, wounded, experienced pain and torment, earlier had experienced hunger, fatigue, sleep. Finally, He tasted death according to the law of man's nature. Why then should one think that, in the case of the Lord, an exception was made only for this side of man's nature, bodily decomposition? Is it rather not true that, in the Lord's humiliation, in His redemptive feat, He took upon Himself all that was human in order to overcome it inwardly, in the nature, not in the symptomatics? In other words, the One who cried on the cross not falsely, "Eli, Eli, lama sabachthani? that is to say, My God, my God, why hast thou forsaken me?" (Matt. 27:46), this One had to follow to the end the way of the cross and of mortality, unto death and decomposition. (It appears that it was precisely this idea that was troubling Dostoevsky's sick imagination, when, in *The Idiot*, he wrote about Holbein's painting, *The Descent from the Cross*.)

Nevertheless, by the Savior's death, death was defeated, despite all the triumph of the symptomatics, for disincarnation, separation of the Spirit and Body did not take place and could not take place, and there was no decomposition and could not be any, for the Body, caught by the divine Spirit and become the entelechic monad of divinity and the center of the whole creaturely world, could now not liberate itself, separate itself from the Spirit. This death was only a symptom, only a state of life, assumed in order to be overcome; just as the "body of sin" was assumed not with sin or for the sake of sin, but in order to overcome sin: "in the grave in the flesh, in hell with the soul as God, in paradise with the thief, and on the throne with the Father and the Spirit art Thou who fillest all things, O Christ the Ineffable."[15] In this sense the Most Pure Body of the Savior can be viewed as the absolute Relic, as the Relic of relics. Nevertheless, the Body of the Lord is not a relic, for It rose from the dead and was taken up from the earth by the ascended Lord. This Body became transcendent to our world, while becoming immanent to it in the sacrament of the Body and Blood. But is it correct to call the Holy Eucharist the Relic of the Savior? No, it is not, because the relics even of saints are nonetheless in a state of separation, of death, whereas the Lord Himself is present in the Body and Blood of Christ.

Sanctifying with Himself all things, the Lord also sanctified the state of holy relics by the fact that His Most Pure Body abided in the grave for three days and three nights in the state of a holy relic, even though It later passed from this state into the state of total resurrection and transfiguration. Thus, if one were to seek a reference point for the veneration of holy relics in the life of the Savior, this point would correspond to the abiding of the Lord in the grave; but that which corresponds to the Resurrection and final glorification of the Body of Christ has not yet come for the world.

We have a perfect parallel in the Dormition of the Most Holy Mother of God. In the Mother of God there is marvelously made incarnate the entire holy essence of our world, whose center She is. And when the body of the Mother of God, after Her Dormition, abided in the grave, it was the Most Holy Relic of the Most Pure One, over whom death had no power in Her capacity as the one "always vigilant in Her prayers and not leaving the world in her Dormition" (from the Akathistos in honor of the Dormition of the Mother of God). But, like the Body of the Lord, the Body of the Mother of God too was taken up into heaven, rose from the dead, and was glorified, which is why one cannot speak of relics with regard to the Holy Body of the Mother of God, although it did pass through the state of holy relics during the three days of abiding in the grave. Thus, this distinction gives us a reference point for that which corresponds to the nature of holy relics in the deification of the world. This is the state of death in which,

15. From the Paschal Hours troparion. — Translator.

however, death has no power: Triumphant on the surface of phenomena, death is powerless in the essence of things; and this powerlessness of death, or the life of the deceased, is precisely the state of holy relics.

This definition requires further elaboration. What is a body from the point of view that concerns us? It is cosmic matter organized by the powers of the human soul which are implanted in it by the act of creation, by the primordial "Let there be." This organization presupposes the conquest of cosmic matter, a spiritualization in the case of which matter is transformed into the state of a body, of a spiritually living essence. That this is so is most clearly evidenced during death, in consequence of which this connection is broken and the laws of chemistry immediately take over: The body decomposes. However, this conquest or penetration of matter is incomplete and insufficient. Between matter and body, and correspondingly between body and soul, there exists not only an indissoluble connection but also a profound disharmony, even an antagonism: The flesh lusts after the spirit and the spirit is enslaved by the flesh. Flesh, as cosmic matter, is disintegration, chaos, atomization, centrifugal force. Between flesh and spirit there was at first established a preliminary and unstable equilibrium, which had to be reinforced by human feat, by human action. But, instead of this, the Fall into sin took place, which shook and disrupted the equilibrium between body and spirit, fracturing the very bond of human organization. By sin entered death, i.e., the morbid, unnatural rupture of this bond, in consequence of which, after death, the spirit finds itself in the unnatural state of disincarnation, while the body again becomes matter, losing the stamp of individuality, spirituality, organization. What is the result? Did the work of the creation of man, of the pneumo-corporeal being, thus come to total failure? Is it the case that man did not withstand his ontological complexity, that the crack that passed through his being resulted in his cleavage and abolition? But this cannot be in the works of God with regard to the crown of creation, who was created as a microcosm. That which took place in man and with man took place also with the whole world. Death, i.e., the insufficient power of life, permeated the whole world; and man, instead of being the bearer of life, became the bearer of death. And it became necessary to save the world and man from death. But this could be done only by pouring into man the power he was lacking — by creating a spiritual body and defeating death. But this was inaccessible and impossible for man in the state of sinfulness; a new creation of man became necessary, with the condition, however, that the old creation be preserved. And this was accomplished by the divine Incarnation of Christ the Savior, of the Savior from sin and from death and, thus, the Savior of the Body.

As true man, He shared the fate of man to the end, i.e., He did not interfere by His divine power with the separation of soul and body, but instead paid to the end His tribute to the state of man. But even for man this phenomenology of death did not correspond to his ontology, for man was created for immortal life with its tasks, although he did not have the power to fulfill them. But here, in the New Man, who was also the True Man, this power appeared; and it appeared not in the embryonic state of naked potentiality, as in the case of Adam, but in the state of perfect and absolute dynamism. In the Savior's death there took place a total contradiction between essence and phenomenon: this Man could not die according to His nature; rather, He died only according to the law of the sinful man, unnatural to Him but taken upon Himself in order to abolish it by Himself. The death here was only a false (for already overcome) and antiquated symptomatics, not death in the strict sense in which it was experienced in sinful man with all its power, but only an episode: the end of earthly, human mortal life, in which, above which, and after which had already begun another life, the immortal life — Resurrection. And this Resurrection has not an individual and episodic nature, but a universally human and ontological one.

Christ rose from the dead in humankind and with humankind: all human beings without exception — because they are human beings, because they are one with Him and have the same nature as He — rose with Him, and death no longer has power over them: death is only the fulfillment of an old, antiquated law, the end of earthly biography, which, in its sum and totality, is only the birth of this new immortal life. It is by the power of Christ's Resurrection that man bears within himself this power of resurrection. In other words, this signifies that death is not at all real, total death, i.e., the complete destruction of soul and body, the destruction of man's ontological foundation, or disincarnation; rather, it is only a swoon of life for the body and, correspondingly, only an incomplete, defective, potential state for the soul. But the victory over death, which had become impossible because of man's weakened powers and required the birth of the New Man, i.e., the divine Incarnation, this victory presupposed, from the human side, that death did not in general have an ontological significance and could not have one, could not completely destroy the connection between body and soul, could not disintegrate matter and subject the human body to full decomposition. This did not happen and could not happen, because by sin it was given to man (as to all creatures) to distort and spoil the human essence, not to destroy it. The power of life, which organizes matter into a body and which was implanted by the Creator, was paralyzed but not eradicated by death. And after death and in death there was preserved the foundation of corporeality, the potency of the body, which is capable of being actualized by the pouring of power into it.

The body must be viewed dynamically, as a kind of dynamic center, a point of application of organizing forces. One can distinguish conceptually and understand occultly,[16] or even physically, this dynamic center of an individual body, but this center remains indestructible, is preserved in the treasure-house of the living forces of nature, in the capacity of numberless seeds of life hidden in nature. It is now time to recall the text that is decisive for our question: 1 Corinthians 15:35-44. This text deals with the same question: If there is going to be a resurrection of the dead, how does one retrieve the bodies that long ago went into the general inventory and material-circulation of nature? Clearly, the question here concerns not bodies, but the material or matter of bodies, matter that is subordinate to time and subject to constant, continuous change, so that, in essence, one can and must say directly that the whole cosmos is matter for bodies, or the common body of humankind. This commonality of body does not, however, prevent the existence of a multiplicity of dynamic centers of this body's possession and organization, just as nothing prevents two men from admiring the same painting or listening to the same symphony.

Clearly, in the case of resurrection from the dead, i.e., in the case of the creation for oneself of a new body, corporealization or incarnation, it is a question not of the matter of a body and its particles eternally flowing

16. See footnote on p. 11.

26

in the ocean of the cosmos, but of the dynamic centers or monads of a body that has a supraphysical and supramaterial character as well as a cosmic character. This is precisely what the apostle Paul speaks about:

> But some man will say, How are the dead raised up? and with what body do they come? Thou fool, that which thou sowest is not quickened, except it die: And that which thou sowest, thou sowest not that body that shall be, but bare grain, it may chance of wheat, or of some other grain: But God giveth it a body as it hath pleased him, and to every seed his own body. All flesh is not the same flesh: but there is one kind of flesh of men, another flesh of beasts, another of fishes, and another of birds. There are also celestial bodies, and bodies terrestrial: but the glory of the celestial is one, and the glory of the terrestrial is another. There is one glory of the sun, and another glory of the moon, and another glory of the stars: for one star differeth from another star in glory. So also is the resurrection of the dead. It is sown in corruption; it is raised in incorruption: It is sown in dishonour; it is raised in glory: it is sown in weakness; it is raised in power: It is sown a natural body; it is raised a spiritual body. There is a natural body, and there is a spiritual body. (1 Cor. 15:35-44)

These divinely inspired words give a new, complete, and blindingly clear answer to the questions that arise here. The mortal body is the *seed* of the future body. But what is a seed or, rather, what makes a seed a seed? Not its material composition, which is destined to decompose, but the mysterious power of the growth, life, individualization, entelechy (using Aristotelian terminology) of the body implanted in it as energy. This energy, which does not exist outside of a given cluster of matter, must nevertheless destroy this cluster if it is to manifest its power. The body is a seed; rather, the body contains the seed of a future body, and this seed is precisely the dynamic center. By His Resurrection the Lord gives the power of growth to the seed, which power will be manifested in the universal resurrection, when there will be as many bodies as there are people or seeds, but, at the same time, the whole world will be one common transfigured body of resurrected man. However, this aspect of the question, important for other questions connected with the cosmism of our existence, does not have significance here, where our attention is directed at the individuality of the body, at the connection that exists between a human being and his body.

This connection is indissoluble and individual, and therefore, as the apostle Paul emphasizes insistently: "all flesh is not the same flesh"; bodies have different glories. But perhaps this difference in glory has a certain basis in difference in death, in difference in dying itself. Here we come directly to the problem of relics. In a certain sense one can say that all of earthly life is a birth, or more precisely a seeding of oneself for eternity — a birth and seeding both of the soul and of the body, in virtue of their fundamental inseparability. That seed of resurrection about which the apostle Paul speaks is not only God's creation, created by virtue of God's omnipotence, but also man's creation, created by the participation of his freedom. Man creates himself, and in particular he creates his own body, stamping it with the stamp of his spirit. And this stamp (the *sragis* of St. Gregory of Nyssa) is the principle of individuality, differing in intensity from individual to individual. Sometimes the stamp is stronger, sometimes weaker. Different spirits master the matter of their body with different strengths, depending on their proper strengths. But, accordingly, it is necessary to conclude that the strength of death differs too. In relation to bodies, death has different strengths. Breaking the union of soul and body, death depersonalizes the body and disincarnates the spirit, although there are objective limits to this destructive work. Nowhere and never is there a total and final rupture, at least after Christ's Resurrection, because all people will be raised in their own bodies, and, at resurrection, the soul will recognize its stamp on the body that will be raised from its own seed: not a new body, but the very same, only transfigured. Thus, the individuality of the body is, in general, ineradicable. The body, as a dynamic center, as a certain bodily entelechy, is preserved in every man, even in the case of its total decomposition. There is no difficulty here to conceive this dynamic body as a potency outside of material actualization.

The greater the spiritual energy, the more distinct this stamping of the body will be, or the stronger the connection of the dynamic body with the soul will be. And in the bodies of saints, in which the decisive victory of the spiritual principle has been won, in which good has triumphed, we do not see that rupture with the body that characterizes total and final death. The bodies of saints retain the acquired power over their dynamic bodies, which have now become spiritual bodies, have acquired the properties of bodies of resurrection.

In a certain sense one can say that saints do not die in the same sense as ordinary people: separation with the body does not occur in saints, for they already possess, even if only embryonically, the body of resurrection prior to the universal resurrection. Their temporal life ends according to the fulfillment of the times and seasons, but they do not know over themselves the whole power of death, after the example of the Lord Jesus Christ, who did not know death to any degree, although He tasted it according to His humanity. The earthly life of saints ends in our spatiality and temporality, but their connection with the world is not broken. Their bodies die, but they do not become corpses, deprived of all power of life. They remain in a special, transfigured state of spiritual body, i.e., they remain holy relics. The seed of the future resurrection of the body, which represents the body of every man, does not die here unto the total swoon of life, as it does among all ordinary men; rather, it preserves life, the warmth and strength of the latter; in this seed, the movement of juices takes place, the mysterious presence of its bearer is accomplished. Holy relics are not corpses; rather, they are bodies of resurrection; and saints do not die; or more correctly, they die in another way, in another sense, to a different degree, than all other people; and, indeed, all people die to different degrees according to the degree they have mastered their bodies. That is the real meaning of the phrase "repose in relics" — which St. Seraphim of Sarov called a special rite or definite state. The bodies of saints, *relics*, are not corpses; rather, they are already transfigured, glorified, holy flesh; they are the altar of the earth, which is why it is natural to place them in church altars, in the most sacred part of the latter (the antimension),[17] as the Altar of altars: they serve as the pedestal of the Body and Blood of Christ. The closeness of saints to us is therefore not only spiritual but also physical (the term "physical" is understood not in a materialistic sense but in the sense of *phusis*, the nature of our world). About saints one can say,

---

17. See footnote on p. 4.

applying to them the words of the hymn about the Lord, that they simultaneously abide in heaven, with the angels at the Lord's Throne (Rev. 7:9ff.), and on earth, both in that world and in this one, both beyond the gates of death and on this side of them. In other words, they retain, in this age too, a connection with their bodies, which death does not have the power to destroy; and it is precisely for this reason and in this sense that they repose in relics, and that holy relics are the object of our veneration in prayer. Holy relics are not the corpses of saints, but their living remains.

Here again there arises before us the question of the remains of saints and their incorruptibility, the question with which we began our discussion. First of all, the remains are not, strictly speaking, the holy relics themselves; they are rather, so to speak, the *place* of the relics, their external shell, or not even a shell, but a cover. The remains are not the very essence of the corporeality, not the integrated spiritual body; rather, they are the material form of the corporeality that the body possessed at the moment of death; in other words, they are not the corporeality in general but the body at a given moment. Of course, we cannot destroy this connection; we cannot consider it accidental or inessential; on the contrary, in conformity with the concreteness of all that exists and the inseparability of noumenon and phenomenon, we must consider the remains of saints to be, so to speak, the phenomenon of the holy relics, and the latter to be the noumenon of the remains. But here we must not forget that not all relics have a phenomenal — for us — existence; some are limited to being-in-themselves, to potentiality. For, in agreement with what we have said, all saints have relics; all of them repose in relics; this is one of the natural consequences and manifestations of sainthood; however, far from all saints have, or have had, relics in the strict sense in which they are the object of veneration. Therefore, the concept of holy relics is both broader and deeper than the concept of the remains of saints. Here, as history attests, remains disappear; they can be destroyed; whereas holy relics are, of course, indestructible. Finally, holy relics are incorruptible in the exact sense of the word, i.e., they have the power of an incorruptible body, inaccessible to death, whereas remains can possess physical incorruptibility (i.e., the delay and slowing of the natural processes of decomposition), not possess it at all, or possess it to different degrees. As is commonly known, the remains of saints have had diverse fates: The bodies of holy martyrs were destroyed by pagans, they were burned or thrown into rivers, and sometimes only small parts of the bodies ended up in the hands of the faithful; then, the bodies of saints were subject to partial or total decomposition, and this as a function of time; and finally, in individual cases, there was an incorruptibility that was miraculous in the sense that it was unexplainable by the usual laws of earthly nature. And therefore, for the sake of precision, it is necessary to distinguish incorruptibility as an immanent quality of holy relics, as their nature, from the incorruptibility of the remains, i.e., of holy relics in the narrow sense of the word.

Holy relics, as remains, *can* possess physical incorruptibility (although, as we pointed out above, only in a relative sense), but they can also fail to possess it, while at the same time possessing the true and immanent power of incorruptibility. Why is that so? The fact of the matter is that this immanent incorruptibility belongs to another order, to another framework of connections, than the causality of the physical world, with its matter. This other framework permeates the physical world, leaving it for a time untouched in its being and intersecting it only at separate points, imparting new properties and powers to it. Relics are fragrant for pious venerators, but this does not at all mean that they possess special perfumes whose particles act upon the nasal region; the fragrance is perceived not outwardly, but inwardly, and therefore it cannot be measured by any external instruments. Likewise, in general the whole power and holiness of holy relics must not be apprehended mechanically; it is accessible only to spiritual experience. In other words, the spiritual body, which is what a holy relic is, can be perceived only by organs (even if only embryonic) of a spiritual body, and not of a physical or "natural" body. The physical or "natural" body, constituting a part of the external world, is subject to the law of the latter; and, as long as this world exists, this body shares the fate of the latter, although this concerns only the crust of phenomena, that which is phenomenal, not that which is noumenal.

Adherents of the simplified understanding of this question — in the sense of the direct physical incorruptibility of holy relics — believe that incorruptibility must in fact consist of the physical undecomposability of the body, but in order to be consistent these adherents would have to insist even on the total unchangeability of the body and its self-identity from the moment of death. In other words, they would have to consider that the entire power of holy relics consists in their physical preservation, and that their entire incorruptibility consists in the unchangeability of the physical body. Such a conception truly suffers from materialism and religious Daltonism;[18] it does not distinguish different planes and different dimensions, and the incorruptibility of holy relics is on another plane, belongs to another dimension, than physical incorruptibility.

The distinctive character of holy relics in this connection can be understood by referring to the Holy Gifts of the Eucharist. In these Gifts we have — more holy even than holy relics — the Most Precious Body and Blood of Christ in the form of bread and wine, substances of this world. For the sacrament of the Holy Eucharist it is essential that these be genuine bread and wine, which constitute the physical matter of the Holy Eucharist. If it is permissible to make comparisons and analogies with reference to things that are so holy, one can say that the bread and wine in the Holy Eucharist represent an analogy to the remains of a body in relation to its relics. The bread and wine are no longer bread and wine; they are transmuted into the Body and Blood of Christ, while preserving the external appearance and physical properties (color, taste, aroma, weight, etc.) of the bread and wine. The miracle of the Holy Eucharist, the love and the divine condescension, are such that they preserve the properties that usually belong to bread and wine. The bread and wine can spoil, so special care must be taken to preserve the Holy Gifts undamaged; in other words, the holiest of all sacraments and transmutation by the Holy Spirit do not offer protection against the forces of natural destruction, against the action of the laws of the physical world. If here there truly must be the appearance of bread and wine (for they are only an appearance, under which the Holy Gifts are offered), this appearance must possess the entire power of its nature and therefore be subject to the action of the forces of nature (water, air, fire). To be sure, the preservation of the physical properties of the matter does not constitute a limit to the power of the Holy Gifts; rather, it is the condition of their offering, established by the Lord Himself.

18. Daltonism is a type of color blindness. — Translator.

The Holy Gifts possess a power surpassing all understanding; but, as long as the existence of this world is permitted, all of its laws must have force, and therefore one should not be offended by the fact that these laws might assume a formula offensive for believers. Nevertheless, without this Eucharistic matter, without the bread and wine, the Holy Gifts cannot be offered — *they do not exist;* there is absolutely no separation between their noumenal essence and their phenomenal manifestation. If the Holy Gifts can be subject to the effect of natural forces and thus do not possess the property of physical unchangeability (or incorruptibility), why should one be surprised or offended by the fact that holy relics too are subject to natural laws and, consequently, to physical decomposition?

One must take both ends of this antinomy in their full significance: the spiritual, incorruptible, supernatural power and essence of holy relics; and the fact that they are a phenomenon in the world and, consequently, are subordinate to the laws of the world. Here, the physical incorruptibility of relics can be only an exception, not a general rule, however this might contradict the conventional view of things. To the extent that it exists, this physical incorruptibility is not supernatural but natural, although, in the broad sense (i.e., the only sense that is rational), a life of holiness could have imparted a greater strength and stability to the physical composition of the body than a life of sin — but that is all. To be sure, holy relics have diverse properties that ordinary bodies do not have; and sensitive natures, or those in a special state that makes them susceptible to such properties, can perceive them. But these properties do not have a decisive significance for the physical preservation of the relics. They are rather the means by which miracles and healings are accomplished, by the action on subtler bodies, especially the effective and inverse action on a physical body. The corruptibility of the remains, which are a kind of storage case for the holy relics, is due to the general corruptibility of matter. Once the death of saints is permitted, then to this extent the decomposition of their bodily remains is permitted. Admittedly, the requirement that the remains be incorruptible is sometimes due not to faith but to lack of faith, which requires a sign like the one demanded from the Savior by the disciples who were thereby called by Him "ye of little faith." It is as if such a purely physical incorruptibility, in itself, is a greater confirmation of the dignity

33

of the holy relics than the general ecclesial consciousness of the holiness and thus of the repose in relics of a particular saint of God.

Incorruptibility means precisely the repose in holy relics, and this is the paralysis of death, the powerlessness of the latter. But the miracle here, which is seen by the eyes of faith, consists precisely in the fact that, in this mortal body, the body of incorruptibility is already contained, is already present, already reposes, inaccessible to our physical senses but manifesting itself as a special presence of the saint who lives here in this body with us and near us. Much more difficult to understand than the corruptibility (always relative) of the remains of saints is their incorruptibility, manifested in many cases and therefore raised to the rank of essential attributes of the remains. This means that, in a given case, among the consequences is the physical preservation of the body as incorruptible. However, this body, although it is incorruptible and visible to us, is not the body of resurrection that lives in the visible body and forms the relic in the proper sense. This is only a cover, like the cocoon that conceals a butterfly. To the extent that this cover belongs to the physical world, it can melt away and become transparent for the body of resurrection. If in a certain sense it is possible to say that it is indeed the body of resurrection, this, ontologically, is indisputably the case, but, empirically, the body preserves its physical mask, which lives according to the laws of physical nature, not spiritual nature. Thus, the remains are only the covering of the holy relics, their raka[19] or receptacle, and therefore they are subject to the laws of this world, and therefore to the laws of death.

And, together with this, it is true that the saint is present in the holy relic, lives in his body, incorruptible and glorified prior to the resurrection; and that is why such a gracious power and help is felt at the raka of a saint, driving into a frenzy the servants of demons and demons themselves, who inspire people to desecrate holy relics. It is for this reason that such power, such protection, such strength and richness are given by the holy places and the abundance of holiness where holy relics repose. For, here on earth, heavenly citizens live with us, among us. If we were worthy, or if it were pleasing to God's will to manifest them to us, we would see them and live

19. See footnote on p. 2.

with them in communion. This indeed is prefigured in the Book of Revelation when it speaks of the thousand-year kingdom of the saints, when their presence and proximity will be felt by those living on earth, and the wall between the worlds will grow thin and become transparent.

Holy relics create for us a physical proximity of the saints, our unearthly protectors — that is the paradox contained in holy relics. Holy relics are inseparable from the remains of the saints and the place of their repose. They are the same thing, and not the same thing; they cannot be identified with the remains of saints, but they cannot be separated from them either. Our theological thought and our sense of piety cannot make this distinction; but even in practice we absolutely cannot make it, because this relationship is outside of our experience. Just as we absolutely cannot and must not separate in the Holy Eucharistic Gifts their holiness of the Body and Blood of Christ from the mold that can form on them according to the laws of the nature of that matter in which they are clothed, so, in similar fashion, we cannot and must not separate or distinguish in practice the holy relic from the corruptible remains; these remains are precisely the holy relics, the incorruptible body of the saint, present among us and living with us. The concreteness of religious feeling, this good and wise fetishism (to use this odious expression once again), does not permit any distinction here, just as there cannot be any distinction according to essence. After all (and here let us not be afraid of a new paradox), the corruption of holy relics, just like the mold and spoilage in general of the Holy Gifts, belongs not to them, but to us; the spoilage occurs *in us,* not in them; when we see and offer this spoilage, we are like those servants of Antichrist who, in poking around in holy relics, brought to light nothing but the spoilage of their own souls. This entire physical phenomenology of holy relics is connected (this is the key point!) not with the relics themselves, but with *our* own state; it belongs to us: we mirror ourselves, we curtain off the other world with ourselves, the veil of Isis is our own materiality, and if we could see and discern in another way, we would see what actually exists, but now we see nothing but our own colored glasses.

But it is impossible to oppose the phenomenon to the noumenon here, or to tear it away from the noumenon; and it is given to us, by condescension to our infirmity and blindness, to venerate holy relics in their corruptible form, which is the only form accessible to us, just as we partake of the Holy Body and Blood — these things of which it is impossible to partake — only in the form of bread and wine.

But, the question might arise, are we ourselves not making the same opposition, by admitting the physical corruptibility of the remains of saints and confessing the incorruptibility of holy relics? This is not a contradiction, however, but an antinomy, in which both sides are equally right and justified: both the thesis and the antithesis, both affirmation and negation. However, this antinomy belongs not to the antinomies of reason, which (comparable to dissonance in music, linking and limiting tonality) ground reason and form the nature of the latter, but to what, like Kant, we can call cosmological antinomies, which refer to and are connected with the *state* of the world. The world lies in wickedness and is subject to death — that is one side of this antinomy, and everything that is in the world is subject to the law of this world; but the world is already saved and redeemed; it contains the principle of incorruptibility; the victory over death has been accomplished. Therefore, there are already two worlds, two principles, two forces in the world; one exists in the other, negating it, but not limiting it in its proper nature.

This antinomic character of the natural world is manifested in the whole of religious-liturgical life and especially in sacraments as supernatural-natural events; and it is this antinomic character of being that explains what is contemptuously and stupidly called fetishism. For, when we venerate an object of the external world, we venerate its supernatural essence; however, this essence is given to us only in the shell of this world, in the material envelope of the latter. Here, the law of identity or self-identity is violated: the object of the external world is unequal to itself and opposite to itself; it is heterogeneous and foreign. He who is perplexed by the incomprehensibility of this or wishes to understand it by means of earthly, "Euclidean" reason, i.e., he who wishes to remove the antinomy, whereas true understanding here can consist only in the most precise statement of the antinomy — he has no business in religion, for the whole of religion issues from this antinomy of the world, from the incompatibility and inseparability of the two worlds.

Thus, we get a series of antinomic propositions: the remains of saints are not incorruptible holy relics, but at the same time they are precisely incorruptible relics, venerated by the faithful. There can be only one practical conclusion from this: the pious veneration of holy relics as having a higher power.

There also follows from this another conclusion, also of primary practical importance: Holy relics possess the property of indivisibility, for the incorruptible body of glory, which they contain, is integral and indivisible; as a dynamic and energetic body, as a "spiritual" body, it does not consist of parts. But, from this, the opposite follows just as evidently: A holy relic can be separated into parts, and each part is the whole relic, i.e., it fully contains it; it is the place of the dynamic, incorruptible, spiritual body; and the physical integrity of the remains, apart from the fact that it is unattainable, does not have any significance (at least with respect to many relics), because the notion of physical divisibility does not have place here. This important practical truth is recognized by the Church when holy relics are divided and parts of them are put into the antimension, with the smallest part having the full power of the whole relic. Here we undoubtedly have an analogy with the Church's teaching about the Holy Gifts of the Eucharist: The Lord Himself is most truly present in each particle of the Holy Gifts. "The Lamb of God is broken and distributed, broken but not divided," says the priest while breaking the Holy Lamb prior to Communion. And this attribute of brokenness and indivisibility also indisputably characterizes holy relics (just as it characterizes holy water, holy myrrh, and other holy objects). The smallest particle of a holy relic has in it the whole relic, which is why the incorruptible body of the saint can be present in particles of the holy relic wherever the latter might abide; and there is nothing essentially incomprehensible in this: After all, even the forces of this world (e.g., electricity) can be manifested everywhere, in many centers. Likewise, it is indisputable that a spiritual body, which is not constrained by our laws of spatiality, can be present simultaneously in many places of our world. The physical concept of holy relics is even broader than that of bodily remains strictly speaking, for holy relics also include garments and other objects which belonged to the saint during his lifetime or which were with him during his burial. If the garments of the holy apostles could heal the sick by being placed on them, this, of course, could in general be explained by the fact that these garments constituted, as it were, a peripheral part of their bodies, i.e., that they belonged among their relics even when they were still alive; for, to be sure, relics are created by life and during life; it is only their manifestation that follows death, and the living St. Seraphim had the same holy relics in his body that are now reposing in the raka.

In connection with this, we must now examine the vexed question, full of temptation, of the counterfeiting of holy relics, supposedly practiced by spiritual speculators among the Greeks and in old Muscovite Russia. In view of the fact that a relic is a dynamic body which chooses for itself a holy relic as its receptacle, it is not absolutely necessary to have documented proof of the authenticity of relics in the sense of establishing that a given part of a relic belongs to the specific remains of a saint. Believers are not commissars; we will not crawl into graves with our analysis; we will not conduct physical studies of holy relics. And, in general, if faith and veneration are present, there is no place or possibility for such studies, which, even apart from all this, would be impossible. Consequently, if pious faith associates the veneration of a particular saint with a particular relic, even if this relic be a product of the severe sin of deception, there is full justification to suppose that the saint being venerated made this relic his own, made it his own garment as it were; and thus we have full justification to consider that what we are venerating here is the actual holy relic of the saint.

However, this supposition must in no way be interpreted to mean that the material shell that houses them has no significance for holy relics. The exception here confirms the general rule; and if we suppose that the saint, because of his love of and compassion for humanity, transforms any little bone into a holy relic, attaches it to his body, this does not at all mean that holy relics can be considered apart from and independently of the remains of the saint. In the *world,* in the cosmic order, holy relics exist and are indestructible, just as their material basis, which is their place in this world, is indestructible, however one conceives this basis (i.e., as an atom-monad or as an energetic center). But, for *us,* holy relics exist only in the appearance, and also under the appearance, of bodily remains; and, in practice, only the remains are relics for us. Therefore (and here we have yet another paradox of the doctrine of relics) holy relics are destructible and can be destroyed, as many of them have been. This by no means signifies their destruction in the world, but it can fully signify their destruction for us. We are deprived of the palpable proximity of the saint and of the veneration of his relics; they become inaccessible for us, depart into another world. *The relics depart* — not from the world (because the essence of holy relics consists precisely in the continuing presence of the saints in the world), but from our field of vision, from us. The servants of the Antichrist have not yet completed the entire program that has been inspired by their fanatical hatred of the Church (and, here, hidden behind them and merging with them are all kinds of heretics and sectarians, Tolstoyans and Stundists,[20] and so on). They have desecrated and profaned the holy relics, demonstrating our powerlessness to protect them. And they have truly demonstrated our powerlessness. If we lose the holy relics, it is because we deserve to lose them. But the goal of the profaners' program is the total destruction of holy relics, which is something fanatical pagans and Jews had carried out in earlier times. We can only speculate about why the profaners have not achieved their goal, but we have not been deprived of holy relics, and must prevent their total profanation by piously and ardently venerating them.

Thus, our discussion has been based on the conviction that the question of the veneration of holy relics is by no means an external and peripheral question, by no means a question that concerns only liturgical and cultic formalities. No, like all cultic questions, it is indissolubly connected with the very essence of the Christian faith. To deny holy relics is to deny the power of Christ's Resurrection, and those who deny them are therefore not Christians. And it is not by chance that the spite and hatred of unbelievers have been directed precisely against holy relics. With their godless and unconscionable protocols and with their profane uncovering of

---

20. Tolstoyans were followers of the moral doctrine of Leo Tolstoy, who evinced contempt for Christian sacraments. The Stundists were a Russian evangelical Protestant sect inclined toward Puritanism and rationalism, and opposed to the doctrine and authority of the Russian Orthodox Church. — Translator.

holy relics, these unbelievers have delivered a painful blow to the hearts of all believers; but the power of this blow, which at first staggered us, must also serve to teach us. We must rise above that low level of dogmatic consciousness thanks to which we so easily pass from sleep and blindness to unbelief and fright; and we must find — first for ourselves and then for the whole community — clear and fundamental answers to the doubts and temptations surrounding this question; and here there is no need to have recourse to random apologetics, or to the negation or fabrication of facts. Once God permitted light to shine into the mysterious half-darkness of the holy place, be this only the light from a prosaic kerosene or electrical lamp,[21] we must not shut our eyes to this light, but rather must calmly and firmly look around. Never of course by our own initiative would we decide to analyze holy relics; never would we decide to peer immodestly, out of curiosity, into the holy raka; but if, against our will, we have been compelled to look, then we must preserve self-possession, understanding, and the faith that sees the invisible in the visible.

21. Bulgakov is speaking of the analysis and desecration of holy relics by Bolshevik officials. — Translator.

On the Gospel Miracles

Author's Preface

In its subject matter, the present essay is a chapter from Christology, and its content can be fully understood only in connection with an integral Christological teaching. However, it can meaningfully stand alone even apart from such a teaching. This essay considers one of the most acute questions of the Christian consciousness in our epoch — the question of human activity in relation to the works of Christ. In the patristic age the works of Christ were primarily considered in relation to His divinity. For us, however, an independent significance is also attached to the question of their relation to His humanity, inasmuch as in Christ's divine-humanity there was undiminishedly united the whole fullness of the divine nature with the whole fullness of the human nature. Dogmatically, we base our interpretation of Christ's miracles on the definitions of the Fourth and Sixth Ecumenical Councils concerning the two natures in Christ, manifested in duality and action and united hypostatically.

I

On Miracle

Miracle occupies a very important place in religious life; for the believing soul it represents, as it were, a proof of God's existence, an action of God in the world. Does not every prayer ask for a miracle? Indeed, for the believer the whole of life is an unceasing miracle that possesses a certain religious self-evidence. However, it is not so easy to express this religious datum in categories of religious philosophy. Even a first attempt to do so makes us see that the notion of miracle can have many meanings and therefore lacks clarity; because of this it can conceal dark superstition and a cowardly lack of faith together with a search for signs condemned by the Lord, but it can also contain the postulate of faith; and in a certain sense it expresses, in general, a religious attitude toward the world. And, first of all, what is the relation of miracle to the cosmic order? Does not precisely this order, the marvelously arranged mechanism of the world with its causality, represent a unique and permanent miracle? And is it not even contradictory to think that, in miracles, the Great Artist Himself abolishes His own creation, completing and correcting it with new creative acts, like a poor master who is compelled to fix a flawed mechanism? This is precisely how this question is posed in deism, which asserts that God stops having any connection with the world after creating it, because such a connection becomes unnecessary, so to speak. However, such a view is based on a faulty understanding of the relation of God to

His creation: It is based on an insufficient, one-sidedly formal understanding of the category of causality.

In general, dogmatics postulates a twofold relation of God to the world: God is considered both as Creator and as Providence. God is the Creator of the world; He created it "out of nothing." Creation is the implanting of the divine, sophianic[1] principles of the world into nothingness, out of which the being of the world arises. This act of God's omnipotence, wisdom, and love — an act unfathomable for the creature and *miraculous* in the most authentic sense — establishes the domain of the extra-divine existence of these principles; and the world, creation, thereby acquires its independence, an existence separate from God. The world is not God, for it is placed outside of God, although it is divine, sophianic in its positive foundation, without which it could not exist, inasmuch as there is no being that does not have its foundation in God. Thus, the world is the extra-divine being of the divine principle, the creaturely Sophia, identical with the divine Sophia in her foundation, but different from the latter in the mode of her existence. The world is the creaturely mirror, the image of the Absolute, the becoming Absolute (to use Vladimir Solovyov's phrase). The creation of the world is the *primordial* divine act, which has the whole power of divine eternity in the infinity of time: "Thou laid the earth on stable foundations, that it should not be shaken for ages and ages" (Ps. 104:5; translated directly from the Russian Bible). This creative act includes the *fullness* and *perfection* and, therefore, the *indestructibility* of the creation. God's creative word, sealed with the life-giving "Let there be," did not resound in time just once like a vain human word, but creates the world in the ages, resounding forever in the universe.

Nevertheless, even though it is unshakably established in its founda-

---

1. "Sophianic" signifies characterized by or emanating from Sophia, the Wisdom of God. Sophia and sophiology are now much discussed in the literature on Bulgakov in particular and on modern Russian religious thought in general. Bulgakov develops his doctrine of Sophia in his Great Trilogy (*The Lamb of God, The Comforter,* and *The Bride of the Lamb,* all published by Eerdmans in B. Jakim's translation). For a clear discussion of Bulgakov's sophiology, see Thomas Allan Smith's introduction to his translation of Bulgakov's *The Burning Bush: On the Orthodox Veneration of the Mother of God* (Grand Rapids: Eerdmans, 2009), pp. xxi-xxii. — Translator.

tion, the world needs, for its own life, divine protection and guidance, i.e., divine Providence. The relation of God to the world as Providence differs essentially from His relation to the world as the Creator. The world received autonomous existence, but this existence is founded upon *nothing*, upon the abyss of nonbeing, which, although it is covered by sophianic being, always threatens, if not being itself, then in any case the fullness of the latter. The world, in its instability, is subject to ontological danger. It is totally incorrect to liken the world to a mechanism, the way deism does. The world is not at all a mechanism; the nature of a mechanism consists in the fact that its structure and its operation are finished and purposive. The world, which at creation received total fullness and total perfection in its ontic foundation, is not at all finished in its state; it is only destined to become the true cosmos, the creaturely Sophia, in virtue of its primordial sophianicity. God has implanted into the world all things that can be *given*, but He has not implanted into it that which it yet has to accomplish for itself. In other words, the world is *becoming*, and becoming presupposes — as the inner foundation of the process — a final goal. The world is not a mechanism, but a living organism, which consists of a hierarchy of entities united among one another, with man at their head as the bearer of free spiritual being; the world also includes the existence and ministry of the angels. *Freedom* is included in the very foundation of the world, which thus is determined not only by its nature but also by the free creative self-determinations and actions of spiritual beings inseparably connected with the world. In the lower and simplest states of being, where there is as yet no place for freedom, what is most distinct is the voice of the world's reason, of the instinctive wisdom of being, of the "world soul" (although, even here, there is no place for mechanism alone). But in the states of being where freedom is manifested, we have the existence of different possibilities, possibilities of the best and of the worst.

Creaturely freedom *makes* the world, which has already been established by God in its foundations; and although, of course, this freedom represents the supreme crowning of the universe, it conceals within itself the dangers of catastrophe. And the double catastrophe of the world in its freedom has already taken place. The first took place in the world of immaterial spirits: This was the Fall of Lucifer and of his angels, a Fall that also threatens the human world. The second consisted in the Fall of man, seduced by the serpent. This second Fall changed the path of the whole of the world's being, for man subjected himself to the flesh, diminished his freedom, and drew the creature into the slavery to corruption, "by the will of the one who subjected it" (Rom. 8:20; the King James Version has been modified). In any case the being of the world is determined not only by the sophianic givenness of the latter, but also by creaturely freedom. There exists here not only natural determinism but also spiritual causality through freedom, with the creaturely creativity characteristic of the latter: Through this connection of the world with spiritual being are indissolubly united spirit and flesh, freedom and necessity, mechanism and creativity. The world is not static; it is dynamic. Not only is it given the sophianic determinism of being, but it also seeks and actualizes this determinism — freely and creatively. But as a consequence of the fact that this life of the world contains different possibilities and dangers, the world cannot be left to itself; it cannot be abandoned without the divine help that it needs. God does not coerce the world in its autonomous being; He does not abolish the real freedom of the world; instead, He interacts with the world, helps it: "My Father worketh hitherto, and I work" (John 5:17).

This is precisely God's Providence for the world. Here, God *interrelates* with the world created by Him as an autonomously existing, extra-divine being not on the basis of creation out of nothing, in the case of which all the activity belongs to the Creator and all the passivity belongs to creation, but on the basis of interaction. God helps the world become itself, without destroying His creation, but nevertheless acting upon it. How can one conceive this interaction of God with the world? Does not its very notion contain an internal contradiction? God, the Creator, interrelates and interacts with His creation — but is not all creation reduced to zero, to the original nothingness, before the Creator, and therefore is it really possible to speak of the interaction of the actual infinitude and absolute omnipotence of God with this nothing, which became something only by His command? Evidently, the creature cannot withstand such interaction, but must be annihilated in the presence of its Creator: The world, like man, cannot see God the Creator face to face without dying. And on the other hand such an interaction of the Creator with creation would signify, in essence, a new creation with abolition of the old creation: It would signify an infinite and continuous re-creation of the world over and over again with a just as continuous destruction of the re-creations, all of which is clearly unworthy of God. Therefore, the interaction of God with the world should be conceived not as a transcendental act of God into nothing, or the creation of the world, but as immanent to the world itself, as an action within creation that does not abolish its autonomous existence and does not violate its indestructibility.

The possibility of such an immanent, providential action of God in the world is based on the fact that the world is characterized not only by a law-governed causality of deterministic being in the self-enclosedness of the latter, but also by spiritual causality through freedom. The causality of the world is not a mechanical predeterminedness of all by all and in all, but a creative actualization of the powers and potencies implanted in it. The world is never closed up in its givenness, but is always in the process of being created, although, in this case, not out of nothing (creation out of nothing is appropriate only to God's original creative act). Therefore, spiritual action is one of the cosmic agents; furthermore, spirit is called in the end to conquer the flesh of the world, to make this flesh obedient to and transparent for it (the spirit): It is called to make the flesh of the world a "spiritual body." But if the world is open to the action of spiritual causality, spirit itself — human and angelic, living and acting in the world — is open to the action of God, to the reception of God's grace, to the reception of power and inspiration. The spiritual causality of the world is precisely the way in which God's *Providence* for the world is accomplished. The spiritual action in the world that is accomplished through man is something we have direct knowledge of. But the world in its entire being is protected and perfected by the ministry of the angels; thanks to this ministry the world, always and in its entire makeup, is open to spiritual action, is not closed off in its material soullessness. The angels are obedient fulfillers of God's commands, although they too fulfill them creatively, as living and free beings, not like mechanical instruments. The holy angels are God's providential will which is being accomplished in the world and over the world. But something similar can be said about man, who too is a spirit, although not an immaterial one, but an incarnate one. Man in his spiritual freedom is a receiver of divine inspirations; through him grace also becomes a cosmic agent, accomplishing God's will in the world. Man is a creaturely god, destined to be deified and thus to lead the world to deification.

Such is the character of the world's conformity to law. On the one hand, the world is determined in its being — in its foundation and limit, in its givenness and in the task it is destined to accomplish, in its creaturely sophianicity, for Sophia is precisely the determinedness of the world. But, on the other hand, the world is not at all determined in the mode of its becoming, in its pathways, for it is a creative, self-creative process which includes causality through freedom. The world therefore contains an infinite number of different possibilities or variants of its pathway, of which only one can become a reality; and God's Providence, by the action on causality through freedom, leads to the selection of the best possibility. Generally speaking, the pathways and limits of spiritual causality are still little known to man, as is also the case with the conformity to law of nature; however, one can say that this possibility is much broader and deeper than we now know. The Lord's words that faith can move mountains express in the form of a parable the general idea that spiritual causality can, within certain limits, command natural phenomena, and wind and waves can be subordinate to it. Here, two pathways of action in the world exist: through cosmic agents or forces of nature, with man acting here as the reason of the world; and in a directly spiritual way, through the subordination of nature to causality through freedom. Both the pathways and the limits of this causality are unfathomable, for it is not limited to the immediate data of a single man but unites him with the entire spiritual world. Therefore, all the departed saints, as well as the immaterial spirits, the entire "invisible church," are included in this spiritual causality and bring down the power of God into the world.

That is also the nature of prayer. In prayer, man addresses God — either directly or through the intermediary of His saints — with a petition that He grant one content or another related to His providential actions in the world, and consequently to spiritual causality in the natural world. Given the limits of human knowledge about such things, not all such petitions are worthy of being satisfied, but every sincere prayer is effective. In prayer, the human spirit opens itself to the actions of God's power; and inasmuch as no prayer is left unanswered, the human spirit receives this power into itself. The action of this power can be accomplished in unknown ways, through God's angels, as well as through the direct action of spirit upon the world, the limits of which action are unknown to us. In any case, prayer belongs to the domain of spiritual action upon the world, to the domain of causality through *freedom;* and therefore it also has a cosmic significance.

But what is miracle? Is it a partial negation and even abolition of cosmic causality, and in such a case what does it signify? Does it signify a new creative act of God that revokes and abolishes the divinely created forces and laws of the world, the divine "Let there be"? Does it represent a correction to, or a completion of, the natural world? Neither religiously nor philosophically is it possible to accept such an interpretation of miracle: It is not possible to accept it religiously because this interpretation does not agree with the fullness and perfection of the creation; it is not possible to accept it philosophically because thought cannot admit a rupture in the causal connection, an interruption in the causal chain. Even if such a rupture could occur, it could not be known by thought. Old Kant is right: In the causal connection of cosmic being everything is given its proper place, and *ex nihilo nihil fit.*[2] But to interpret miracle as a new creative act of God, as a kind of divine coercion over the life of the cosmos, is tantamount to interpreting it as appearance *ex nihilo.* And against such nihilism, which abolishes the power of cosmic being in favor of the miraculous, logic imposes a prohibition with its protective principle of causal connection: *causa aequat effectum,*[3] or the same principle in a negative form, *sublata causa, tollitur effectus.*[4] Miracle cannot be understood as something without cause; it must occupy its place in the causal series, even if only as a special case of causality. Causality is the logos of the world, the law of which is the continuous logical connection of all with all. In the causal series or more precisely in the infinite causal series that expresses this universal connection, we have causes of different character, including causality through freedom.

2. Out of nothing, nothing comes. — Translator.
3. Cause equals (originates) effect. — Translator.
4. When the cause is removed, the effect ceases. — Translator.

However, all of these different causes are equally cosmic, are included in the life of the cosmos, can be understood on the basis of this life.

Miracle is just as cosmic and law-governed as all natural phenomena. The character of miracle consists not in causelessness or supracosmicity, but only in a *special* causality; and in the final analysis, in relation to the cosmos, miracle must be judged to be natural, not supernatural and especially not unnatural. In other words, miracle refers not to the creation but to God's Providence for the world. But God as Providence acts in the world not by coercing it, not by correcting or changing the principles of its being, but only by guiding, through spiritual causality, the world's natural, or mechanical (so to speak), causality. This *union* of spiritual causality (through freedom) and mechanical causality (through necessity) is what constitutes the character of the law governing the cosmos. The world is not a mechanism, but rather an organism, growing and living. This connection of spirit and nature (here, the spirit can be subordinate to and enslaved by the flesh, but the flesh can also be obedient to the spirit), this spiritual-natural structure of the world constitutes the permanent miracle of the world, the miracle of miracles as the foundation of all that is miraculous. Here, in the domain of spiritual causality, we have two opposite possibilities: At one pole we have the corruption of mankind when it becomes "flesh" (Gen. 6:3), and at the other pole we have the spirit-bearing glorified flesh of Christ together with the spiritual body of resurrected mankind (1 Cor. 15:44, 46) and together with the transfigured heaven and earth. The character of spiritual power in the world can vary, for the freedom of creaturely spirits is capable of being directed either upward or downward, either toward God or toward the world, either from God or against God, both in the angelic and in the human world. From this come two inspirations, dark and light, and two orders of miracle (in the sense noted), good and evil, or true and false. But both orders of miracle occur in the world, take as their foundation the powers and possibilities of the world. About the apocalyptic beast it is said that "he doeth great wonders, so that he maketh fire come down from heaven on the earth in the sight of men, and deceiveth them that dwell on the earth by the means of those miracles which he had power to do in the sight of the beast" (Rev. 13:13-14). The apostle Paul says the same thing about the wicked one, "whose coming is after the working of Satan with all power and signs and lying wonders" (2 Thess. 2:9). True miracles, i.e., works of love and faith, are accomplished by the power of the creaturely spirit, aided by God's grace.

The distinction between true and false miracles consists in the fact that true miracles are manifestations of the *spiritual* mastery of the world through spiritual causality according to God's will, and lead, in the final analysis, to the deification of the world through the communion of the latter with the God-Man by the power of Christ; whereas false miracles signify the appearance of human power in the world without the mastery of it with God's help. Such false miracles are cases of natural magic, which is based on "knowledge" and the concentration of will within one's ego, on oneself and in oneself. This magic, which is accessible to men in varying degrees, is often equated with miracle. One cannot deny, of course, that magic, i.e., the power over nature that is an inherent property of man, is present in miracle. By contrast, spiritual causality is in general accomplished by the power of man's spiritual action in the mechanism of the world. Thus, it is possible to distinguish two types of magic: "white" magic, which works true miracles, and black magic. Magic that works signs is white magic (a good biblical example is the transformation of a rod into a serpent worked by Moses in the name of God), whereas the same thing done by sorcerers is black magic. Magic has different modes of being; our contemporary science also becomes a magic when its goal is to regulate the forces of nature. It is precisely science that in our day is becoming more and more like both white and black magic. Science is accomplishing true miracles, works of love and mercy, but at the same time it is serving human egotism, pride, and evil passions. In itself, magic (i.e., man's power over nature) belongs to man from his creation; it is connected with his dominant position in the world and cannot be taken away from him, although its pathways can differ.[5] Man is in fact created to become the creaturely god of the world.

5. It is worthy of note that, in the case of the temptations in the wilderness, the devil tempted Christ with the power of false signs, i.e., with black magic, promising Him the power to transform stones into bread and to overcome the weight of His own body; but the Lord rejected this as a temptation, for *in its purpose* this represented black magic, false signs. But Christ Himself — when He multiplied the loaves of bread, walked on water, etc. — worked the same signs as true miracles in the name of God.

Spiritual causality in the natural world, manifesting the naturalness of the latter, can be accomplished by different pathways, direct and roundabout. Let us take an example. Someone heals an infant dying from diphtheria by the spiritual power of his prayer; this is an example of the direct pathway of spiritual causality, which alone is usually called a miracle (although, in essence, it does not contain more of the miraculous than any other human action in the world). In another case, a doctor uses medication to heal the infant. Is that a miracle too? Undoubtedly, for one who does not know the possibilities of medicine, such a healing is as much a miracle as a healing without the use of medication. The result is the same in both cases, but the pathway is also the same: spiritual causality, the *action* of man upon the forces of nature. The difference lies only in the means of action: In one case, the action takes place *within* nature itself, while in the other case it takes place *from outside,* as it were; but of course in reality the miracle worker too does not accomplish a new creative act and even does not change the laws of nature, but only gives them a new direction by his spiritual power. His spiritual action becomes a physical force, as it were — but only "as it were." In essence, in both cases we equally have the action of spirit upon the forces of nature, i.e., we have an action that directs or regulates. In both cases we have the action of man in the world through spiritual causality; in both cases we have the manifestation of human power in the world. The difference consists perhaps only in the fact that, in one case, we have the manifestation of the personal power of an individual human being, while in the other case we have the *common* work of all humankind, which includes the contribution of individual human actions. One can say that the first case has only an "indicative" significance, attesting to man's vocation and indicating the path he should take, while in the second case we have the path of all of humankind, for man is a member of humankind which has its common work in the world. Both paths are possible and, speaking abstractly, compatible. However, historically, one path keeps waging a quarrel with the other. Having entered the age of technological and scientific miracles, humankind has less and less need of personal miracles as pathways of power over the world; and consequently the very notion of miracle acquires more and more a moral or spiritual character, losing its natural character.

The person of the miracle worker is more miraculous for us than the miracles themselves. The greatest Gospel miracle is Christ Himself, His person, His preaching; in general the phenomenon of the God-Man is a greater miracle than the individual Gospel miracles. The most shattering and ineradicable impression is produced on us by the image of the suffering Christ, when He is no longer working miracles — i.e., by the image of Christ as the revelation of God-Love in man. The seeking of miracles as signs, to replace or to get around the laws of nature already known to us and living in us, is superstitious and unhealthy; and it was repeatedly condemned by the Lord, who more than once told those who sought miracles from Him: "An evil and adulterous generation seeketh after a sign; and there shall no sign be given to it" (Matt. 12:39; cf. Matt. 16:4; Mark 8:12; Luke 11:29-32); and here He precisely indicates His preaching and His ministry (Matt. 12:41-42). Nevertheless, in the life of every man who carefully examines his spiritual life there constantly occur miracles, which, however, do not revoke natural laws but fully conserve them. Miracle is a phenomenon of divine purposiveness in the world. And our desire for miracle comes down to the desire that our life be lived according to God's will, which is revealed in our life. And in this sense, truly, the life of every believer, for him himself, is full of miracles, is an unceasing miracle.

II

The Miracles of Christ

In thinking about miracle, we naturally and inevitably come to the Gospel narratives about Christ's miracles, for, just as in the true humanity of Christ we recognize ourselves, so in Christ's miracles we seek to recognize the power given to us over the world. If the greatest miracle of Christ is He Himself, His Person, then His appearance as prophet and as miracle worker consisted first of all in spiritual power and authority, which was revealed both in word and in deed: "He taught them as one that had authority" (Mark 1:22). "And they were astonished at his doctrine: for his word was with power" (Luke 4:32). "And many hearing him were astonished, saying, From whence hath this man these things? And what wisdom is this which is given unto him, that even such mighty works are wrought by his hands?" (Mark 6:2). The Gospel miracles represent, as it were, a self-evident manifestation of this power. It is characteristic of the Gospels to avoid using the word "miracle" with reference to Christ's acts: *teras* is used only by way of exception; the word most commonly found in the Synoptics is *dunamis* (power), while John usually employs *semeion* (sign). Furthermore, in the Gospel of John the Lord sometimes just uses the word *erga*, the works that bear witness to Him (John 5:36; 10:25). These works, "which none other man did" (John 15:24), consisted of preaching, healing, good works.

Before examining these miracles, let us first pose a general dogmatic question: What were the miracles in Christ's ministry? Were they caused by divine action or by human action? Was it God or was it man in the God-Man who worked these miracles? Were they creative acts of God's omnipotence, which created the world; or were they manifestations of the power of perfect Man? This was precisely how this question was posed in the dogmatic teaching, and the solution to this question consisted in affirming that, as God, Christ worked miracles by divine power, whereas, as man, He was weak with human infirmity.[1] We will not examine in detail this Christological opinion, which in a hidden form contains the Nestorian separation of the two natures in Christ. Having two natures, two wills, and two "energies," Christ nevertheless had one human *life*; and the separation of His life into two would attest only to the Nestorian *sunatheia*,[2] not to the unity of His hypostasis. Therefore it is necessary to exclude the idea that Christ performed some of His works (or individual parts of some of them) as God, while performing others as Man: such a mosaic of the two natures is inadmissible. Being the God-Man, in the unity of His Person He performed all works and experienced all things with both the divine essence and the human essence, of course in conformity with the nature of each of them. Therefore, to entirely exclude the participation of the divine essence in some manifestations of His life (in particular, even in His sufferings), just as to exclude the participation of the human essence in some of them, would be to separate Christ in a Nestorian manner and even, in place of a moral unity of *sunatheia*, to establish some sort of queue of two in one, as if the sundering into two of His Person, which cannot be. On the contrary, it is necessary to postulate the *continuity* of the life, will, and activity of the *two* natures in Christ; this is the self-evident postulate of the dogmas of the Fourth and Sixth Ecumeni-

---

1. This is what we read in Pope Leo the Great's epistle to Flavian: "One of them shines with miracles, while the other is subject to humiliations. To hunger, to thirst, to become fatigued and to sleep, this, evidently, is proper to the man. But to feed a multitude of five-thousand with five loaves of bread, to give living water to the Samaritan woman, to walk on the surface of the sea with unsinking steps, to tame the tempest, this, without any doubt, is proper to God. . . . It is not proper to one and the same nature to weep from sorrow over a dead friend and to raise him from a four-day grave with a commanding word."

2. Conjunction without true unity. — Translator.

cal Councils (the dogmas of the union without separation and without confusion of the two natures, and two wills and energies in Christ). In application to Christ's miracles, it is necessary to establish that they were performed by the God-Man in the hypostatic union of His divine and human natures. Therefore, being "signs" of divinity, His miracles were also human and therefore cosmic in character, representing a revelation of man in the world; and it is this human cosmicity of Christ's miracles that we are attempting to clarify here.

Christ's humanity was (contra docetism) authentic, even though it encompassed the fullness of divinity bodily. His humanity belonged to the world and carried within itself the life of the world. Christ's miracles were the works of a Man who, having the Logos as His hypostasis, encompassed within His life the fullness of divine vision, divine knowledge, divine life; the humanity of Christ which was united without separation and without confusion with His divinity was deified, so that the Son of Man was also the Son of God, "the only begotten Son, in whom I am well pleased." But in all of this the perfect humanity was not abolished and not dissolved, but revealed to the end. Christ is the Son of Man, and His acts — and in particular His miracles — are human works, although ones that are accomplished in full conformity with God's will. According to the dogma of the Sixth Ecumenical Council concerning the two wills and two energies in Christ, Christ worked miracles both as God and as man. The divine side of this miracle-working is, of course, unfathomable for created beings. However, we can ask whether this divine side refers to the activity of God the Creator, who calls completely *new* creations out of nonbeing, or whether it refers to divine Providence, which provides for the world that is already created and existing, the world that is finished and has its own laws in its natural being. The divine Logos is the One "by whom all things were made; and without him was not any thing made that was made" (John 1:3); He is the Creator of the world, who called the world out of nonbeing and maintains it in its being. By the Logos was also created that very same humanity which was assumed by Christ in the capacity of His human nature; and this assumption of the human nature attests that the creation has been completed and is assumed by the Logos in its perfect form: *kai ho Logos egeneto* (John 1:14). The creation of the world, which in

God takes place in God's eternity, for the world took place in a single primordial pre-temporal act, which began time and is continuing in the latter as it were, filling all time. It follows that the Incarnation of the Logos as an event in the world and in the temporal being of the latter is not a creation of the world but belongs to the domain of God's providence for the world, to the domain of the interrelation and interaction of the Creator with the creature. Of course, the Incarnation of the Logos occupies the central place in God's providential plan; and in relation to the world the Incarnation has the significance, as it were, of a new creation, or more precisely of the re-creation of the world, the making of it anew through the appearance of the perfect Man who is also the God-Man; but even this re-creation presupposes a creation that has already taken place. Therefore, the Logos in Christ is revealed not as the Creator of the world, who laid the foundation of the latter and maintains it by His might, but as Providence, existing in a definite interrelation with the world (which, in particular, is expressed also in the union of the two natures, divine and human, without confusion and without separation).

Therefore, likewise, the character of the divine participation of the Logos in the working of Christ's miracles must be understood as a providential action of God in the world, where, however, the autonomy of the latter is preserved. Consequently, from the divine side, miracles are not a new creation; they are acts not *upon* the world, but the action of God *within* the limits of the world, directing the life of the latter. Nor can miracles be understood as a new creation of the world, even if only in an infinitesimal part of the latter, because that would already mean the creation of a new world by the introduction into it of a system of new elements and by the destruction of the unity of elements already existing in it. The creation of only a single new atom in the world already changes the whole world. And since the world recognizes itself in man, who is a "contracted world,"[3] the new creation or change of the world introduces a change in man too — and here humanity itself loses its stable definition, changing with each miracle, which serves as a new ontic impetus. From this it would appear to

3. A reference to Nicholas of Cusa's doctrine that each thing in the universe is a contracted or compressed form of the latter. — Translator.

follow that miracles change even the humanity of Christ, assumed by the Son of Man from the old Adam in all fullness and authenticity (see the genealogy of Christ in Luke 3), but this is obviously impermissible. Thus, the ontological stability of the world turns out to be a condition, and also a consequence, of the divine Incarnation itself.

Therefore, from their divine side as well, Christ's miracles cannot be understood as creative acts of God upon the world, or as a new creation, but rather refer to the *providential* action of God in the world, are immanent to the world, are accomplished within the limits of the possibilities of the world or within the limits of the forces implanted in the latter. And it is precisely the providential character of miracles (which corresponds to the fact that on the seventh day God rested from His works, having finished and exhausted *creation*) that makes understandable the interrelation of the divine and human natures in Jesus during the working of miracles. If, Christologically, it is impossible to affirm that Christ worked miracles only by divine power (this would be Eutychianism, which asserts that the humanity in Christ is swallowed up by His divinity), there is also no theological necessity to affirm this. If we attempt to understand miracles as acts of a new creation, they would clearly belong only to God, they would be works of His omnipotence, and man would not participate at all here. Christ's human nature, itself being a creation of the Logos, would then, at most, remain passive in working miracles. The presence of His human nature would not have any significance for this creative action of the Logos, and it would even be ontologically shaken by these creative acts, which would represent jolts of its being, as it were. But if miracles are providential acts of God in the world and upon the world, to which Christ's own humanity belongs, there follows from this the full possibility and even necessity of the co-participation in these miracles of the human nature as belonging to this world, for they are not miracles in the sense of a new creation but only manifestations of *powers and signs* in this world. This interrelation of the divine and human natures in Christ which we see in the working of miracles is the same that has place in the entire life of the God-Man. The divinity, which has humbled itself to the point of incarnation and which in this kenosis has concealed its greatness and omnipotence as if in potentiality, nevertheless inspires with itself the entire human life of the God-Man. The humanity, undiminished in its autonomous being and freedom and retaining the entire human life ("will and energy"), is constantly inspired by the divinity, is deified in full measure ("for in him dwelleth all the fullness of the Godhead bodily" [Col. 2:9]), so that every human act is also a divine-human, deified act, and nothing occurs outside this intercommunion (*communicatio idiomatum*[4]).

Therefore, Christ's miracles were worked by the Son of Man, and they were worked by Him in His humanity; consequently, they have a human character, are accessible to man, are included in the possibilities of this world, headed by man. This means, furthermore, that Christ's miracles were *natural*, not unnatural and not supernatural. They disclosed the possibilities implanted in man's relation to the world. They represented humanity's testimony about itself, for man is called to be the "lord" of the world; he is the king of creation, the creaturely god. And this power of man over the world is attested in the perfect Man with staggering force, although (it is necessary to add at once) miracle-working is not something that belongs to Him alone but is, in general, proper to many spirit-bearing men of the Old and New Testaments. From the fact that the miracles are worked by Christ with the participation of His humanity, it follows that all of them have a human character, i.e., are accessible to man and are possible for him. Their miraculousness consists only in the special manner of their working, extraordinary for the given conditions; e.g., the healing of sicknesses is in man's power, and miraculous healings differ not in their purpose and their essence but only in the extraordinary means by which they are achieved. Not all the works related to miracles are at present accessible to man, but this does not mean they will be impossible in the future: "He that believeth on me, the works that I do shall he do also; and greater works than these shall he do" (John 14:12) — that is the general interrelation that is established in the words of the Lord Himself. *All* miracles are, in essence, accessible to man; and all of them (even the raising from the dead) were already worked by the Old Testament prophets, by Moses, Elijah, and Elisha. Christ gives the apostles the power to perform

---

4. Communication of properties. A patristic term expressing the interchange of properties between divinity and humanity in the God-Man. — Translator.

all miracles when He sends them off to preach: "Heal the sick, cleanse the lepers, raise the dead, cast out devils" (Matt. 10:8; Mark 3:15; Luke 9:2); and the disciples "cast out many devils, and anointed with oil many that were sick, and healed them" (Mark 6:13). Of course, the Lord would not have given this command, which contains the fullness of His own miracle-working, to His apostles (and in their persons to the whole Church, which is clear from His words after the Resurrection: Mark 16:17-18), if these works did not have a human character, if they were not accessible to man. It is these very miracles that we see performed by the apostles after the Resurrection (as described in the Acts of the Apostles); these include many healings and even raisings from the dead. And this gift of miracle-working continues in the Church in all times. All this confirms that the working of Christ's miracles belongs not only to His divinity but also to His humanity; and consequently His miracles were worked humanly, through the disclosure and actualization of human possibilities.

In the Gospel this human character of Christ's miracles is confirmed indirectly as well. The Lord attested that "this kind goeth not out but by prayer and fasting" (Matt. 17:21) and He Himself prayed when He worked miracles. This is attested directly only about certain individual acts: before walking on the sea, during the course of a night He prays alone (Matt. 14:23); when feeding the multitude, He looks up at heaven and blesses the bread, i.e., He prays (Matt. 14:19; Mark 6:41; Luke 9:16). At the Transfiguration, "as he prayed, the fashion of his countenance was altered" (Luke 9:29). And, finally, when performing the most staggering miracle — the raising of Lazarus — the Lord prays to the Father, as is clear from His words: "Father, I thank thee that thou hast heard me. And I knew that thou hearest me always" (John 11:41-42). Even this miracle, which theologians usually attribute to the divinity alone ("as man, Christ wept; as God, He raised from the dead"), was worked by the power of prayer, to be sure by human prayer, for prayer is proper to the God-Man in His humanity.[5] And

---

5. Therefore, it is impossible to accept the opinion of John of Damascus, who (in the *Precise Exposition of the Orthodox Faith*, IV, XVIII) says that "Some things Christ did for the sake of appearance: for example, when He asked where Lazarus had been laid (John 11:34), when He approached the fig tree (Matt. 21:19), when He prayed (John 11:42). He had need of such things neither as God nor as man; rather, He acted humanly, for the sake of appearance,

this power of prayer, in the capacity of spiritual causality in the world, is expressed by the Lord in a generalized manner in the words of the Sermon on the Mount: "Ask, and it shall be given you ... for every one that asketh receiveth ... your Father which is in heaven [will] give good things to them that ask him" (Matt. 7:7-8, 11), as well as, of course, in the Lord's Prayer, this Prayer of prayers. There is a second feature in Christ's miracle-working that speaks about its human character, with reference to both the subject and the object: This is the participation in the miracle not only of the one who works the miracle but also of the one who receives it. For the vast majority of the miracles the condition of their working is *faith*, because of which and in conformity with which the miracles are worked: the healing of lepers (Mark 1:40-41; Matt. 8:2-3; Luke 5:12-13); the raising of the daughter of Jairus (Mark 5:22-23; Luke 8:41, 50; Matt. 9:18); the healing of the possessed (Mark 9:25-27; Matt. 17:18); the healing of the blind Bartimaeus (Mark 10:52); the healing of the centurion's servant in Capernaum (Matt. 8:8-10; Luke 7:6-9); the healing of the woman with an issue of blood (Matt. 9:20-22; Mark 5:25-29; Luke 8:43-48); the healing of the two blind men (Matt. 9:27-30); the healing of the daughter of the woman of Canaan (Matt. 15:22-28; Mark 7:25-30). If we compare the various narratives we will become convinced that all of these cases bear special witness to faith as causing or accompanying the miracle. But even more expressive are cases with an opposite character, when the absence of faith is an obstacle to the working of a miracle or, at least, to the reception of it. Such cases are directly attested to in the Gospel: "And he could there do no mighty work, save that he laid his hands upon a few sick folk, and healed them. And he marvelled because of their unbelief" (Mark 6:5-6); "and he did not many mighty works there because of their unbelief" (Matt. 13:58). These texts, in which skeptics see evidence that the miracles were accomplished by virtue of the faith of those healed (by virtue of autosuggestion) but could not occur if it were absent, represent in reality only a confirmation of the essential human character of the miracles. Miracles are not a violence done to the world but represent a disclosure of the proper powers and potencies of

_____

where need and usefulness demanded it; for example, He prayed in order to show that He was not God's opponent, but rather venerated the Father as His Cause."

the world, with *both* sides participating in this disclosure: not only the worker of the miracle but also the recipient of it. Miracles are worked not only *ex opere operato* but also *ex opere operantis*.

It is remarkable that even in the miracle of the raising of Lazarus we see the presence of this feature, namely the participation of faith, although, of course, what operates here is not the faith of the man who died but the faith of his sisters (similarly, the faith that operates in the case of the raising of the daughter of Jairus is the faith of the father): "Then said Martha unto Jesus, Lord, if thou hadst been here, my brother had not died. But I know, that even now, whatsoever thou wilt ask of God, God will give it thee" (John 11:21-22); and the first half of these words is repeated by Mary (11:32). Through faith they became participants in the raising, just as in other cases when miracles were worked through faith and could not be worked without this condition. Thus, in a certain sense one can say that miracles are a *common* work of humanity, not the work of the miracle worker alone.

Let us now look attentively at the particular features that accompany the working of different miracles. An enormous number of miracles are worked by *word* alone, the direct action of the Lord's command, direct spiritual causality. This applies also to many prophetic and apostolic miracles in both the Old and New Testaments. First of all and most naturally, healings of the possessed are accomplished in this way. But however we interpret such possession, as demon possession or as a neuropsychic illness, or as both, the word is the direct and effective instrument both for the commanding of demons and for psychic suggestion, which even in our own era is employed by medical practice in the form of hypnosis. The word, uttered with power, is in this case the natural means for acting upon unclean spirits who sense from afar the approach of the Son of God ("And, behold, they cried out, saying, What have we to do with thee, Jesus, thou Son of God? art thou come hither to torment us before the time?" [Matt. 8:29]) as well as upon the psyches and nervous systems of sick persons (through suggestion and autosuggestion). But, apart from this, an enormous number of Gospel miracles are worked by the Lord's direct command through word, in some cases through word that responds to faith and unites with the latter, and in other cases through word that directly commands: Simon's wife's mother (Luke 4:39); the leper (Luke 5:12-13); the man sick with the palsy (Luke 5:24-25); the man with the withered hand (Luke 6:8-10); the healing of the centurion's servant in Capernaum (Luke 7:1-8); the raising of the son of the widow of Nain (Luke 7:14-15); the healing of the ten lepers (Luke 17:14); the healing of the daughter of the woman of Canaan (Matt. 15:22-28); the healing of the man with the infirmity at the pool of Bethesda (John 5:8-9); the healing of the son of the nobleman of Capernaum (John 4:50-53). Related thereto are miracles worked by word of command directed at nature: at wind and sea (Mark 4:39-41; Luke 8:22-25; Matt. 8:23-26); at the fig tree (Mark 11:14, 20); in the case of the miraculous catch of fishes (Luke 5:4-7). There are analogies in the Old Testament: Moses' miracles at the exodus from Egypt and during the wandering in the desert; and the miracles of the prophets Elijah and Elisha.

However, there is a whole series of miracles where the Lord does not limit Himself to word alone but performs certain actions that are the *means,* as it were, for miracle-working. Thus, when raising the daughter of Jairus, "he took the damsel by the hand, and said unto her, Talitha cumi" (Mark 5:41); when healing the man who had an impediment in his speech, Jesus "took him aside from the multitude, and put his fingers into his ears, and he spit, and touched his tongue; And looking up to heaven, he sighed, and saith unto him, Ephphatha, that is, Be opened" (Mark 7:33-34). The healing of the blind man is described in the following way: "And he took the blind man by the hand, and led him out of the town; and when he had spit on his eyes, and put his hands upon him, he asked him if he saw ought. And he looked up, and said, I see men as trees, walking. After that he put his hands again upon his eyes, and made him look up: and he was restored, and saw every man clearly" (Mark 8:23-25). In other cases the miracles were worked by *touching:* the most expressive case was the healing of the woman who had an issue of blood: "When she had heard of Jesus, [she] came in the press behind, and touched his garment. For she said, If I may touch but his clothes, I shall be whole. . . . And Jesus, immediately knowing in himself that virtue had gone out of him, turned him about in the press, and said, Who touched my clothes?" (Mark 5:28-30; Luke 8:44-46; Matt. 9:20-21). But "the whole multitude sought to touch him: for there went virtue out of him, and healed them all" (Luke 6:19). "Now when the sun was setting, all they that had any sick with divers diseases brought them unto him; and he laid his hands on every one of them, and healed them" (Luke 4:40). It was by touch that He healed the ear of the servant of the high priest (Luke 22:51). The healing of the man blind from his birth was accomplished in the following manner: Jesus "spat on the ground, and made clay of the spittle, and he anointed the eyes of the blind man with the clay, and said unto him, Go, wash in the pool of Siloam. He went his way therefore, and washed, and came seeing" (John 9:6-7). (We find analogous cases of healing through touch in the Old and New Testaments, particularly in Acts 5:15-16; 9:11-12.) These cases are characterized by the fact that the Lord did not limit Himself to word or command but performed certain *actions*, which were miraculous means for the accomplishment of His will. The miraculous feeding of a multitude of 5000 by five loaves of bread and of a multitude of 4000 by seven loaves was accomplished in an analogous manner: namely, the Lord "took the seven loaves and the fishes, and gave thanks, and brake them, and gave to his disciples, and the disciples to the multitude" (Matt. 15:36; Mark 8:6-7; cf. Matt. 14:19; Mark 6:41; Luke 9:16; John 6:11). The Lord worked this miracle by prayer ("looking up to heaven") and by blessing.

How are we to understand this distinction in the mode of working of different miracles? Should we understand it to signify different manifestations of God's omnipotence, which is not associated with any external means of action and, as if bearing witness to this indifference, uses different means?[6] We have already rejected the understanding of miracle as a new creation, and by no means do these texts contain grounds for confirming it. In the actions of the Lord when He healed the man blind from his birth, it is by no means necessary to see a new creation of an eye out of the earth. Such an understanding of miracle would rather destroy its significance for man, reducing it to a game played by the omnipotence, to a kind of *deus ex machina.* Such, by the way, are the miracles that are attrib-

---

6. In certain individual features some perceive the direct likening of individual miracles to a new creation worked by God, in particular the healing of the blind man through spitting and of the man blind from his birth by means of clay from the earth: in order to repair certain damaged parts of the human body, God again creates the body of man out of the earth.

uted to Christ in the "Gospels for children," which have been justly rejected by the Church (e.g., the bringing to life of birds molded by Him out of clay). Would it not be more correct to recognize that, when working miracles, the Lord in certain cases considered word alone to be insufficient or unsuitable, but used certain external actions as well, which were *means* for the working of the miracle? These means were miraculous in the sense that people did not understand them; but the important thing is that they were included by the Lord Himself in the mode of the working of the miracle. In this we see a confirmation of the general idea that the Lord's miracles have a human, cosmic, natural character; that they remain in interaction with the world, are immanent to the latter. As miracles they are manifestations of spiritual causality, of divine Providence. However, inasmuch as they are natural and possible in nature, the mode of their accomplishment is determined by their naturalness. Therefore, it turns out that in some cases the *suitable* means for miracle-working is the word; in some cases it is touch or the laying on of hands (i.e., bodily action); in some cases it involves the use of matter of the physical world (e.g., clay and spittle); and, finally, in some cases it involves the combined action of prayer and personal participation in the breaking and distribution of loaves of bread. The essentially important thing here is not the means in themselves (because all of them are equally obedient instruments in the hands of the Lord), but the fact that the Lord Himself gave them a place in His miracles, thereby demonstrating that they also have a natural-human character.

*   *   *

Let us now turn to the *content* of Christ's miracles, in an effort to establish what was in them and what was not in them. The first thing that strikes us is the fact that, of the total number of Christ's miracles depicted in the Gospels, the vast majority are healings; furthermore, even though a significant number of these healings are described separately, many more do not receive individual mention but are only noted as occurring in mass healings. The Lord is depicted as a miraculous healer surrounded by the sick in body and soul, by the possessed, by lepers, by men with palsy, by blind men, and so on. Human sorrow and suffering is present before Him in all its helplessness and hopelessness; and He "pities" this human sorrow and suffering, and helps this suffering humanity. We repeatedly find the following picture in the Gospels: "And great multitudes came unto him, having with them those that were lame, blind, dumb, maimed, and many others, and cast them down at Jesus' feet; and he healed them: Insomuch that the multitude wondered, when they saw the dumb to speak, the maimed to be whole, the lame to walk, and the blind to see: and they glorified the God of Israel" (Matt. 15:30-31). In the land of Gennesaret, "when they were come out of the ship, straightway they knew him, and ran through that whole region round about, and began to carry about in beds those that were sick, where they heard he was. And whithersoever he entered, into villages, or cities, or country, they laid the sick in the streets, and besought him that they might touch if it were but the border of his garment: and as many as touched him were made whole" (Mark 6:54-56). "Now when the sun was setting, all they that had any sick with divers diseases brought them unto him; and he laid his hands on every one of them, and healed them" (Luke 4:40). "But so much the more went there a fame abroad of him: and great multitudes came together to hear, and to be healed by him of their infirmities. And he withdrew himself into the wilderness, and prayed" (Luke 5:15-16). The general impression from the appearance of Jesus among the people is expressed by these words of the Gospel of Matthew: "And Jesus went about all Galilee, teaching in their synagogues, and preaching the gospel of the kingdom, and healing all manner of sickness and all manner of disease among the people. And his fame went throughout all Syria: and they brought unto him all sick people that were taken with divers diseases and torments, and those which were possessed with devils, and those which were lunatick, and those that had the palsy; and he healed them" (Matt. 4:23-24). The same idea is expressed more concisely in the apostle Peter's speech to Cornelius: "How God anointed Jesus of Nazareth with the Holy Ghost and with power: who went about doing good, and healing all that were oppressed of the devil; for God was with him" (Acts 10:38). The Lord manifested compassion toward suffering humanity; He had pity on it. According to His immaculate and perfect humanity, He Himself was free of all these sicknesses and sufferings, which entered into the world as a consequence of original sin, but the Son of Man by His compassionate love took upon Himself the sufferings of others, as this is noted by the Evangelist: "When the even was come, they brought unto him many that were possessed with devils: and he cast out the spirits with his word, and healed all that were sick: That it might be fulfilled which was spoken by Esaias the prophet, saying, Himself took our infirmities, and bare our sicknesses" (Matt. 8:16-17).

On the background of this general healing and these good works the individual cases of healing that are highlighted in the Gospels represent only singular episodes, which are mentioned because of one peculiarity or another; however, all of these acts are works of human mercy and compassion, human works accomplished according to the will of God. Compassion for human sorrow is what inspires the working of another category of miracles — the raising of the dead. This is directly stated about the raising of the son of the widow of Nain: "And when the Lord saw her [the widow], he had compassion on her, and said unto her, Weep not" (Luke 7:13), and He raised the young man. The raising of the daughter of Jairus was accomplished in order to fulfill his request that his daughter be healed: "My daughter is even now dead: but come and lay thy hand upon her, and she shall live" (Matt. 9:18), and when the young girl died, "all wept, and bewailed her: but he said, Weep not" (Luke 8:52). This too was of course an act of compassionate mercy toward human sorrow. But the same thing must be said about the raising of Lazarus. Faithful to the general character of his Gospel, the Evangelist John, it is true, underscores the symbolically triumphant aspect of this miracle as a "sign of victory" over death, as a manifestation of God's glory (John 11:4, 40-42), but this does not at all diminish its aspect as an act of compassion toward the sorrow of the sisters of the deceased, a sorrow that was shared also by those close to him (11:19, 31, 33) and by the Lord Himself, in whose case this human sorrow is expressed with particular power: "Jesus wept. Then said the Jews, Behold how he loved him! . . . Jesus therefore again groaning in himself cometh to the grave" (11:35-36, 38). In this sense the Gospel raisings can be said to belong to the large general group of miracles of healing and philanthropy, inspired by compassion and mercy, by the desire to lighten human sorrow, to make human life easier and less sorrowful, to help suffering humanity. And it is remarkable that in the vast majority of cases the Gospel narratives do not indicate any particular reason for the working of the miracles, or for choosing the recipients of the miracles. We do see, it is true, a series of cases where the miracle is requested by or offered in response to ardent faith, but, as a rule, healings are accomplished upon *all* the suffering people Christ encounters on His path. Suffering as such is sufficient occasion for His acts of compassion. Not even the Lord's last miracle, the healing of the ear of the servant of the high priest (Luke 22:49-51), constitutes an exception to this rule. "And there came a fear on all: and they glorified God, saying, That a great prophet is risen up among us; and, That God hath visited his people" (Luke 7:16; cf. John 6:14).[7] The feeding, occurring twice, of the multitude in the desert has the same significance of mercy and compassion (apart from its symbolic significance as a prefiguring of the Eucharist). The story of the feeding of a multitude of 5000 with five loaves of bread is told in Matthew 14:14-21 in the following context: "And Jesus went forth, and saw a great multitude, and was moved with compassion toward them, and he healed their sick. And when it was evening, his disciples came to him, saying, This is a desert place, and the time is now past; send the multitude away, that they may go into the villages, and buy themselves victuals. But Jesus said unto them, They need not depart; give ye them to eat." This context is even more expressive in Mark 6:33ff.: "And the people saw them departing, and many knew him, and ran afoot thither out of all cities, and outwent them, and came together unto him. And Jesus, when he came out, saw much people, and was moved with compassion toward them, because they were as sheep not having a shepherd: and he began to teach them many things. And when the day was now far spent, his disciples came unto him, and said, This is a desert place . . ." etc. We have the same thing in relation to the feeding of a multitude of 4000 with seven loaves of bread: "Then Jesus called his disciples unto him, and said, I have compassion on the multitude, because they continue with me now three days, and have nothing to eat: and I will not send them away fasting, lest they faint in the way" (Matt. 15:32). We find the

---

7. In this same category of miracles we can place the manifestation of the power of healings given to the apostles, about whom it is said: "they cast out many devils, and anointed with oil many that were sick, and healed them" (Mark 6:13).

same thing in Mark 8:1-3: "In those days the multitude being very great, and having nothing to eat, Jesus called his disciples unto him, and saith unto them, I have compassion on the multitude, because they have now been with me three days, and have nothing to eat: And if I send them away fasting to their own houses, they will faint by the way: for divers of them came from far." Thus, this miracle too has the significance of compassion, of care for human needs.[8] If we divert our attention for a moment from the miraculous character of this feeding, we can say that the Lord simply wished to feed the hungry and those in want, that he did not neglect the bodily needs of the people, but manifested care and compassion, that He *pitied* the people (this human feeling for suffering humanity, and for Christ Himself, will be asked of us as well at His Dread Judgment). And the impression produced on the people by this miracle was similar to that produced by His healings: "Then those men, when they had seen the miracle that Jesus did, said, This is of a truth that prophet that should come into the world" (John 6:14).

Among the miracles of philanthropy, of compassion toward human suffering, we can include a miracle performed out of sympathy for human joy: the transformation of water into wine, which is narrated in the Gospel of John as the first miracle, the "beginning of miracles" (John 2:11); and it is characteristic that this beginning[9] is dedicated to human joy (although this entire narrative in John has, of course, a symbolic sense saturated with meaning).

When one subtracts all of these miracles of mercy and compassion, all these works of the Lord's love, from the total number of Gospel miracles, there remain only five miracles that do not belong here, but occupy a singular place. These miracles are: the walking on the sea, the taming of the tempest, the finding of the didrachma in the fish's mouth, the miraculous catch of fishes, and the cursing of the fig tree. The trait common to all of these five miracles is that their purpose is to teach the disciples and to

---

8. Here too the Evangelist John uses this event as a prefiguring of the Eucharist.

9. From this it follows, by the way, that the Evangelist does not consider the recognition of the Lord in the souls of the apostles — in Peter (John 1:42) and especially in Nathanael (1:49) — to be one of Christ's miracles.

influence their souls. The first miracle, the taming of the tempest (Matt. 8:23-27; Mark 4:35-41; Luke 8:22-25), has a symbolic significance as a trial of the disciples' faith, as well as a manifestation of Jesus' power over the elements: "What manner of man is this, that even the wind and the sea obey him?" (Mark 4:41). The second miracle, the walking on the sea (Matt. 14:25-27; Mark 6:45-51; John 6:17-21), has a similar significance, as does the miraculous catch of the fishes (Luke 5:6-9). The Lord's command to find a piece of money in the fish's mouth (Matt. 17:27) has the same symbolic significance: It is a kind of real symbol. In these miracles the Lord *teaches* His disciples not only by word but also by deed, pouring His lessons into their hearts. However, these particular cases are swallowed up by the total mass of Christ's miracles that represent works of love and mercy; and it is this feature — love and mercy — that defines the fundamental character of Christ's miracles, their profound *humanity* and *love of man*.[10] And in this sense the Lord Himself solemnly defines His works twice: the first time is in His first preaching in Nazareth, where He directly applies to Himself Isaiah's prophecy (Isa. 61:1-2): "The Spirit of the Lord is upon me, because he hath anointed me to preach the gospel to the poor; he hath sent me to heal the brokenhearted, to preach deliverance to the captives, and recovering of sight to the blind, to set at liberty them that are bruised, to preach the acceptable year of the Lord" (Luke 4:18-19). The second time is in the answer to John the Baptist through the latter's disciples (also using the words of the prophet Isaiah): "Go and shew John again those things which ye do hear and see: The blind receive their sight, and the lame walk, the lepers are cleansed, and the deaf hear, the dead are raised up, and the poor have the gospel preached to them" (Matt. 11:4-5; cf. Isa. 29:18; 35:5-6). In the Gospel of Luke (7:21), here is the preparation for this narrative: "And in

---

10. In conformity with its general theological character the Gospel of John in the narrative of the miracles too indicates the divine nature of the Lord as well as the special symbolic significance of "signs," in accordance with which almost every miracle is followed by a teaching on the occasion of this miracle, by a theology of this miracle, so to speak. We find such a "theology" after the healing of the man with an infirmity (John 5:17-47), after the feeding of the multitude with five loaves of bread (6:26-58), after the healing of the man blind from his birth (9:3-5, 39-41), and of course after the raising of Lazarus (11:25-27). In the Gospel of John we also have a general doctrine of Christ's works.

that same hour he cured many of their infirmities and plagues, and of evil spirits; and unto many that were blind he gave sight."

The Lord manifested *powers (dunameis)* in his miracles, and these manifestations were also *signs (semeia)*, but He did not work miracles in order to blind and subjugate people, depriving them of their spiritual freedom. The Lord speaks with reproach (to the nobleman of Capernaum): "Except ye see signs and wonders, ye will not believe" (John 4:48). It is worthy of attention that Christ's miracles, while teaching some, only hardened the hearts of others, and this is shown with particular clarity in the entire Gospel of John, and especially with reference to Christ's most startling miracle — the raising of Lazarus, after which Christ's enemies decided to put Him to death (John 11:53). It is this feature that distinguished Christ's miracles from those false miracles whose purpose is to blind and enslave man and, in general, to manifest power not in the name of the love of God and man but in the name of pride and self-glorification. Of particular significance in this sense is the Lord's reproach to the people: "Ye seek me, not because ye saw the miracles, but because ye did eat of the loaves, and were filled" (John 6:26). It is such miracles that satan tried to induce Christ to perform during the temptations in the desert; and it is such miracles — "signs" (in the bad sense) — that the Pharisees repeatedly tried to induce Him to perform (Matt. 12:38-39): "Then certain of the scribes and of the Pharisees answered, saying, Master, we would see a sign [*semeion*] from thee. But he answered and said unto them, An evil and adulterous generation seeketh after a sign; and there shall no sign be given to it, but the sign of the prophet Jonas" (cf. Matt 16:1-4; Luke 11:29-31). This is even more expressive in the Gospel of Mark (8:11-12): "And the Pharisees came forth, and began to question with him, seeking of him a sign from heaven, tempting him. And he sighed deeply in his spirit, and saith, Why doth this generation seek after a sign? verily I say unto you, There shall no sign be given unto this generation."

When the Lord worked miracles, it was not in order to enslave people with superstitious fear and, in general, to make these miracles the instrument of His power in the world and in His kingdom. In connection with this it is necessary to understand a fact that immediately strikes one's eyes: In the Gospels the overwhelming majority of the miracles refer to the *first* part of Christ's earthly ministry, with the number of miracles gradually decreasing as the time of His suffering approaches. The first boundary here is the event on the way to Caesarea Philippi and the confession of Peter, after which the Lord reveals to the disciples that He has come for suffering. It is true that this was followed by the Transfiguration, and then by the healing of the possessed and a few individual miracles (the piece of money in the fish's mouth, the healing of the blind man of Jericho, and the final general healing in the Temple of "the blind and the lame [who] came to him" [Matt. 21:14] after the Lord's entry into Jerusalem), but the miracles are noticeably replaced by preaching, by parables and discourses. At the threshold of the sufferings there is the miracle-sign of the raising of Lazarus and then the cursing of the fig tree, and then the final miracle, the healing of the slave's ear. At the time of the Passion *the miracles ceased.* It was precisely at this time that they could have been "signs," worked for the sake of His protection, but the Lord rejected such protection: "Thinkest thou that I cannot now pray to my Father, and he shall presently give me more than twelve legions of angels?" (Matt. 26:53). (This is a reference to God's providential activity, accomplished through the angels.) And it was precisely at this time that the demand for signs with which satan had tempted Christ was repeated with particular insistence by the Jewish leaders: "let him now come down from the cross, and we will believe him. He trusted in God; let him deliver him now" (Matt. 27:42-43). But the Lord, the Lover of man, who worked miracles in the name of the love of man, here, for the sake of that same love of man, does not protect Himself against death on the cross. In connection with this there arises the general question which is constantly posed in Christology in relation to Luke 2:40, 52, which speaks of the human growth and strengthening of Christ, and of His increase in wisdom and stature.

In interpreting this text some of the fathers do not consider it possible to allow the true growth and development of Christ in His humanity, whereas others do allow it. We consider that it conforms to the truth to accept a divine Incarnation in the case of which the human nature is subject to *temporal* development, i.e., to accept the *human* development of the Lord to the point of fullness and perfection (just as it is said about us: "Till we all come in the unity of the faith, and of the knowledge of the Son of God, unto a perfect man, unto the measure of the stature of the fullness of Christ" [Eph. 4:13]). But in connection with this it is necessary to pose the question concerning the fulfillment of His human power with reference to His miracle-working (if the latter is not attributed, as some theologians do, wholly to the divine nature, but we have already rejected this). It appears that, with reference to miracle-working, one must accept the presence of development in a sense that cannot be defined precisely. In confirmation of this one can adduce the general fact that the Gospel does not tell of any miracles performed by Jesus in His childhood (although the apocryphal Gospel is full of them), boyhood, or youth (this idea is only indirectly confirmed by the narrative of the conversation with the rabbis in the Temple, which reveals the nature of His intellect). The miracles appear only at the beginning of His ministry, and, together with the preaching, they are an indication that He has attained fullness of powers and maturity. We do not have the ability to establish any change in the power of the miracle-working (or of the preaching) as a function of internal causes, first of all because there does not exist a strict chronological framework in the Gospels and, secondly, because Christ's acts are also defined by the relation to Him of the people, with the growth of the inevitable conflict. It is impossible to avoid the impression, noted primarily by unbelieving historians, that there exists a difference between the beginning and the end of the Lord's ministry, although this difference does not disrupt the unity of this ministry: The beginning of the ministry passes in more radiant and joyous tones than the second part of it, with the growing tragedy; and accordingly, the Lord's words, which previously were merciful and forgiving, become severe, pitiless, and judging (see the last discourses of Christ according to the Gospels of Matthew and Luke). Although we cannot establish any differences in Christ's miracle-working power, we cannot avoid the idea that the miracle of the raising of Lazarus, in its triumphant and symbolic character ("assuring us of the universal resurrection prior to Thy passion, Thou, Christ God, raised Lazarus from the dead," is what the Church hymn says), represents, in a sense, the pinnacle of miracle-working, and also its limit — within the bounds of the Savior's earthly life, prior to His salvific Resurrection (when "He is already given *all* power in heaven and on earth"). To this is added the impression that this miracle demanded a special intensity of human powers as well, a special exertion of the Savior's will; and in the lengthy narrative of the raising we witness, as it were, this exertion and struggle. Still being some distance away from Lazarus, He tells His disciples: "Our friend Lazarus sleepeth; but I go, that I may awake him out of sleep" (John 11:11), thus manifesting His will toward his raising, and also attesting that, as in the case of the raising of the daughter of Jairus ("the maid is not dead, but sleepeth"), this is not death without awakening, but only a swoon of life, which only appears to man to be death, although it really passes into the latter. And then He once more confirms that this is His will, telling the disciples: "Lazarus is dead. And I am glad for your sakes that I was not there, to the intent ye may believe; nevertheless let us go unto him" (John 11:14-15). Thus, He is already going to Lazarus with the purpose of raising him. After this is described Jesus' own agitation and sorrow, and the description is one of extraordinary power: "When Jesus therefore saw her weeping, and the Jews also weeping which came with her, he groaned in the spirit, and was troubled" (11:33); and then, "Jesus wept" (11:35); and finally, "Jesus again groaning in himself cometh to the grave" (11:38). We witness here the intensity and growth of Jesus' human sorrow and compassion. This is followed by the greatest intensity of prayer, which concludes with the certainty that the prayer has been heard and fulfilled: "Jesus lifted up his eyes, and said, Father, I thank thee that thou hast heard me" (11:41); this is followed by the working of the miracle. It appears to us totally impossible to accept here a "Nestorian" separation of the natures and their alternation, to accept that as man, He wept, but as God He raised Lazarus; to accept that the man promised the raising, but the God accomplished it. All of it was the work of the God-Man in the unity of His hypostasis and in the duality of His natures, i.e., it was not only a divinely providential work but also a humanly accomplished one, and we are present at this miracle which is a manifestation of God's power revealed in human will. In the narrative of John 11, the miracle of raising from the dead is depicted not only from the external but also from the internal side, as it was accomplished by Christ Himself; and it becomes clear that this supreme miracle is also the *final* miracle, the limit to human power *on this side* of the Resurrection of Christ.

In the Gospel of John, the Lord usually speaks of His works (*erga*) in a general sense. And, first of all, He attests that with His works He does the will of the Father: "The Son can do nothing of himself, but what he seeth the Father do: for what things soever he doeth, these also doeth the Son likewise. For the Father loveth the Son, and sheweth him all things that himself doeth: and he will shew him greater works than these" (John 5:19-20; cf. 10:25, 37-38). This passage speaks, on the one hand, about the intratrinitarian interrelation according to which the Son reveals the Father and has nothing in Himself that is His own, not His Father's; and on the other hand it says that Jesus' human will is totally obedient to the divine will revealed in Him. "The works which the Father hath given me to finish, the same works that I do, bear witness of me, that the Father hath sent me" (John 5:36; cf. 14:10-11): this was the Lord's answer to Philipp (cf. 15:23). The main idea being developed here is that, in virtue of the unity of the Father and the Son, the works of the Son are also the works of the Father: "If I had not done among them the works which none other man did, they had not had sin: but now have they both seen and hated both me and my Father" (15:24). And, addressing His disciples, the Lord says: "Believe me that I am in the Father, and the Father in me: or else believe me for the very works' sake. Verily, verily, I say unto you, He that believeth on me, the works that I do shall he do also; and greater works than these shall he do; because I go unto my Father" (14:11-12). The works here are, first of all, a revelation of God the Father and the Son, of divine love for human beings; and, secondly, they are works in the proper sense, i.e., accomplishments, and an expression of the truth of human divine-sonhood. God gives us the power to become children of God who believe in the Name of Christ (John 1:12), and by virtue of this divine-sonhood the sons of God receive the power to do the works "that I do," and even greater works, for Christ has gone to the Father. Thus, here the works are not miracles alone, but the *whole* vocation of man in the world as the son of God, as the creaturely god. This idea marks the transition to the final and most important question concerning Christ's miracles, the question of their significance *for man.*

III

On Human Works

What do Christ's miracles signify? Of what are they the *signs,* and of what are they the *powers?* They are the signs of God's love for man, for God so loved the world that He sent His Son into it. And they are manifestations of God's power in man, works of the Son of Man and the Son of God, the God-Man. In their content miracles are works of love and mercy; in their significance they are manifestations of human power in the world, human power that is reinforced and illuminated by God's power. Being divine according to inspiration and providential will, miracles are *human* works, performed within the limits of the world and of humanity. The healing of spiritual and physical sicknesses in man, unto the healing of death through at least a partial victory over it — these are the works which, as signs, are contained in Christ's miracles. These tasks are *human* tasks, and these works are *human* works; and all of them are accessible to man, are assigned to him as a natural being, who at the same time is placed by God as the lord of creation and endowed with the gift of compassionate human love for man and for all creatures. If we ignore the particular miraculous means required for their accomplishment, all of these works are human works. It is true that not all of them are capable of being accomplished by human powers. Man is not yet able to eliminate death by natural means and to awaken people from the swoon of death, although he is approaching this; nor has he yet eliminated hunger, although he is seeking means to do so, and all this is something that does not surpass human powers. The proof of this is that all of Christ's miracles, in their content, could have been worked by divinely inspired saintly men, strengthened by God's grace; and consequently these miracles belong to the category of human power, to the category of man's lordship over the world, given by God to man at his creation. The expulsion of demons? But even if we ignore the story of Tobit in the Old Testament, the New Testament Church, beginning with the apostles, possesses this power to such an extent that it has a special gift and ministry of exorcists (a ministry that had special bearers in the early Church and that nominally is still preserved in the Catholic Church); and if one understands this to mean the treatment of sicknesses of the soul, this has been the business of medicine and psychiatry from time immemorial. The healing of sicknesses? But we have it also in the Old Testament (the healing of the leper Naaman by the prophet Elisha, etc.); and the New Testament Church is full of "healings," so that the apostle Paul calls "healing" a gift among other gifts (see 1 Cor. 12:9, 30): the healing of the lame man (Acts 3:1-8); the healing of the sick and the possessed by the shadow of Peter (Acts 5:15-16), and by the handkerchiefs or aprons of the apostle Paul (19:11-12).

The raising of the dead? But this too is given to man, for in the Old Testament the prophet Elijah raised the son of the widow in Zarephath of Sidon (1 Kings 17:17-24); Elisha raised the son of the Shunammite (2 Kings 4:17-37); and the man who was being buried came back to life just from the touch of the bones of Elisha (13:21); in the apostolic Church, Tabitha is raised by the apostle Peter (Acts 9:36-41), and Eutychus is raised by the apostle Paul (20:9-12). Belonging to this category are miracles of the saints, for example, the healing of the youth by St. Sergius. Finally, the Lord Himself gave the commandment to the apostles, and in their persons to the whole Church: "Heal the sick . . . and raise the dead" (Matt. 10:8) The miraculous feeding, with the multiplication of the loaves of bread? However we understand this event, i.e., whether we see in it primarily a natural miracle of the multiplication of loaves or an impulse based on love to divide among ourselves whatever is present according to Christ's blessing, we must in any case remember that this miracle too has a parallel in the Old Testament: the multiplication by the prophet Elijah of a handful of meal and a little oil that belonged to the widow in Zarephath of Sidon, which fed her and her house for many days (1 Kings 17:12-16); the miracle of the increase of oil worked by the prophet Elisha in the house of the widow, and especially the miraculous feeding of one hundred men by twenty loaves of barley, with loaves left over (2 Kings 4:1-7, 42-44); and also the transformation of a poisonous pot of pottage into a harmless one by the addition of a handful of meal (4:39-42). Power over the forces of nature, over wind and sea? But in the Old Testament we have, besides the plagues of Egypt, the crossing of the Red Sea (Exod. 14:21-29), the miracles of Moses in the desert, the falling of the walls of Jericho from the sound of trumpets (Joshua 6), the prophet Elijah's bringing fire down from heaven onto the sacrifice (1 Kings 18), the separation of the waters of the Jordan worked by the prophets Elijah and Elisha by smiting them with a mantle (2 Kings 2), and the miracles of Elisha involving the healing of waters by a handful of salt (2 Kings 2:19-22), the punishment of the children by having them torn apart by two she bears (2 Kings 2:23-24), and the rescuing of the axe from water (2 Kings 6). In the New Testament Church, witness is borne to various miracles from the domain of man's power over nature (in particular, the walking of St. Mary of Egypt on the waters of the Jordan); one should also not forget that Peter walked on water by Christ's command and began to sink only when he got frightened (Matt. 14:28-30).

What does this comparison of Old and New Testament miracles tell us? Does it diminish the uniqueness of Christ's miracles, which consists not in the miracles, but in the Miracle Worker Himself as a manifestation of the Perfect Man? No, it does not, but it shows perfectly clearly the erroneousness of the theological idea that Christ's miracles were worked by divine power alone, as if apart from His humanity and its powers. All of the miracles cited were worked by holy *men*, although, of course, with God's aid. This comparison shows once again the *human* character of Christ's miracles, compels us to see in them a *revelation of the perfect Man*. They do not surpass the measure of man in his original state and calling. "I have no man" (John 5:7), exclaims the man with the infirmity before the Man who will heal him. We will now explore this human character of Christ's miracles.

And, first of all, it is necessary to establish the *naturalness* of these miracles in the sense that all of them constitute not a violation or revocation of the foundations of the universe laid at the creation, but a disclosure and application of these foundations. They are supernatural only in the sense of the special mode of their actualization, through the direct application of spiritual causality, but not in the sense of their content. All of them are accessible to man in the sense that they can and must constitute a task for him as well, irrespective of the means of their actualization: whether miraculously, i.e., by direct spiritual causality, by the spiritual power of man over nature, which, though it has been weakened by original sin, nevertheless still belongs to man to a certain degree (yoga!); or through the application of the forces of nature, known by human reason, i.e., also, in the final analysis, by spiritual causality. This is the power of man over nature, applied out of love of man. In fact, is man not able and obligated to heal sicknesses of various kinds, and does he not do so? And are all the possibilities of this already exhausted, or, on the contrary, do they keep increasing in number? Will this healing, which is of course a struggle with death, although one that does not defeat it but only delays it, will this healing not reach a point where it will be able to snatch away from the claws of death its untimely victims? Although this is not yet possible, mankind has already started out on the path to such a conquest of nature. Does not the feeding of the multitudes by all possible means, just like the multiplication of the loaves of bread, i.e., an increase in the total quantity of goods necessary and possible for man, does not such feeding constitute a constant human concern crowned by increasing achievements? Finally, does the conquest of the forces of nature in the most general sense also not constitute a constant aspiration of mankind, which here is actualizing the Lord's command: "subdue it [the earth]" (Gen. 1:28)?

In other words, all of the "works" of Christ can be directed at human will as an example and summons, or as a "project" (to use Fyodorov's[1] term). And this is the primary and most direct meaning of the Lord's words about His works: "He that believeth on me, the works that I do shall he do

---

1. The "project" of the Russian philosopher Nikolai Fyodorov (1828-1903) was expounded in his main work, *The Philosophy of the Common Task*. According to this project, it is man's task to aid God in the work of resurrection by developing technological means to raise from the dead all the human beings who have ever died. With the abolition of death, the ultimate goal is the transfiguration of humanity and then of the entire universe. — Translator.

also" (John 14:12). Rationalistic prejudice denies Christ's miracles because they are "physically impossible": it considers these works to be impossible because they contradict the laws of nature, and belief in them (as well as the reports about them in the Gospels) presupposes the absence of scientific knowledge of the laws of nature. And, conversely, for superstition the laws of nature simply do not exist in relation to miracle: Miracle takes place outside and above these laws. Setting aside the imprecision with which particular miracles are reported (the sacred writers never aimed to describe miracle as a physical experiment), we can say about men of rationalistic prejudice that their judgment is self-assured and limited. It appears to them that the present state of knowledge has already exhausted all the possibilities of nature, whereas in truth it is only discovering these possibilities, and the domain of the naturally possible is expanding to such a degree that one cannot assert with scientific conscientiousness that any particular miraculous event is physically impossible and unnatural. By contrast, the superstitious understanding of miracles errs by disrespecting God's creation and its laws, insofar as this understanding considers anything at all to be possible irrespective of the world's laws. Such anticosmism in the understanding of miracle makes the latter alien to man, dehumanizes miracle so to speak, and contradicts the fact that the miracle-working Lord is God and Man with two wills and two energies. At best, man here is only a passive instrument, through which God's power acts. Thus, it is necessary to understand miracle as a natural and human event, i.e., as a manifestation of natural law acting through man.

But what then does miraculousness in general consist in? It consists in its purposiveness; spiritual causality, emanating from the human spirit and the freedom of the latter, is transparent in miracle. But by no means is spiritual causality unnatural, for it is included by the Creator in the very foundations of the natural world. Man is a natural agent who perceives and awakens the reason of nature, and employs this reason for his own purposes — for the humanization of nature. In *this* sense of spiritual causality in nature through freedom, all human activity is miracle. But there exist different levels of this human activity in nature, and we distinguish certain of these levels in virtue of their express purposiveness, which consists both in the elevated character of the purposes and in the special energy with which they are actualized; and we call these levels miracles. Man is an incarnate spirit, which means that the unity of natural and supernatural being is actualized in him. His supernatural being is divine in its origin (for God Himself breathed the soul into Adam), whereas his natural being is destined to be deified through the implanting into him of God's grace; and let it be noted that, in Christ's humanity, this deification was accomplished in absolute measure, for His incarnated hypostasis is the divine Logos Himself, and upon His human nature the Holy Spirit Himself descended in the Baptism. However, the action of spirit in the world through man, spiritual causality, is limited by the creatureliness of man, who does not create the world himself but has it as a given with its laws: these laws are the condition for the life of man and for his activity in general, for the manifestation of spiritual causality in the world. Man's spiritual causality in the world is, however, limited by the state of fallen man, who through sin weakened his spirituality and the power of his influence in the world in the sense of spiritual causality, and lost his lordship over the world, becoming not its master but its enchained slave, although he is still called to freedom and to action in the world through spiritual causality. The Lord in His inhumanization, in virtue of the genuineness of the latter, accepted the inviolability of this world with its proper laws, which for Him too constituted a *given*, albeit a given that was willingly accepted by Him. As perfect man, the Lord manifested in the world the whole fullness of human givenness unweakened by sin, and in this He was truly Man: *"ecce homo."*

True, having entered the world, which was damaged by the sin of Adam, and having received flesh, which, although it was sinless, was weakened in that it was afflicted by the infirmities that afflict men (hunger, thirst, fatigue, suffering, even death), the Lord actualized this perfect humanity by the way of the cross of His earthly life, ascending from power to power. He possessed nature to a unique and exclusive degree, according to the power of His perfect humanity. These were precisely the miracles of Christ, *dunameis*, the powers that were manifestations of man's lordly position in the world, albeit in conformity with the nature and laws of the latter. *"Gratia naturam non tollit, sed perficit"* (Thomas Aquinas).[2] It cannot be said

---

2. "Grace does not destroy nature, but perfects it." — Translator.

that the Lord, by virtue of omnipotence, worked *all* miracles in general, actualizing in them all the possibilities that are inaccessible to ordinary human powers. As is clear from our earlier analysis of Gospel miracles, they were, in essence, very limited in their range and did not represent "signs" of the manifestation of omnipotence; in a word, they were not a violation of the life of the world. The Forerunner said (using an anthropomorphic trope) that "God is able of these stones to raise up children unto Abraham" (Luke 8:3). But did the Lord make people out of stones? Did He transform women into men? Horses into donkeys? Did He move mountains? Did He bring fire down from heaven? And so on. In general, did He work miracles for the sake of miracles? The fact that He did not is another indication of the great simplicity and limited nature of the Gospel miracle-working. With His miracles the Lord indicates the possibility of man's spiritual action upon nature, but by His example He does not have in view to exhaust or limit the sphere of these possibilities. This is precisely what He means when He says: "He that believeth on me, the works that I do shall he do also; and greater works than these shall he do" (John 14:12). The task of doing His works He entrusted to His humankind, indicating the path and revealing the possibilities, but not limiting them. And these "greater works," these possibilities, include the conquest of the world, or, using Fyodorov's terminology, "the regulation of nature," a task man has already begun. The human pathways of the conquest of the world are something man has to find in himself and through himself, because these pathways are implanted in him at his creation; and all creatures, for their own becoming, are waiting for man to accomplish this conquest. By His miracles Christ indicates to man the pathway of power over the world through the humanization of nature, not the pathway of flight from and hatred for the world. How is it that people have still not seen this! They have not seen it, they have not heard Christ's summons, only because His miracles have been viewed solely as a manifestation of His divinity.[3]

---

3. We have a de facto Monophysitism which passes over into an Apollinarianism in the following statements of John of Damascus (from the *Precise Exposition of the Orthodox Faith*, III, XV): "The power of the miracle-workings was an action of His divinity. But the works of His hands, and the fact that He willed and said, 'I will; be thou clean' (Matt. 8:3), were an action of His humanity. The breaking of the loaves of bread, and the fact that the leper heard 'I

However, man's place in the world is not determined solely by his connection with nature and his relation to nature's laws. Man is a natural phenomenon, a fact of natural life, like a stone, a tree, and so on. Like all things, he is subject to the laws of this world, and in this respect he does not differ in any way from other things. That is how materialism assesses man. But such a meager understanding of man is possible only if we look at him from outside, as at a thing, closing our eyes to his actual life, which is determined by the presence of a living and creative spirit in him. This spirit is ontologically inseparable from man's body and, in and through the latter, it is inseparable from the world. Man is therefore the creative principle in the world, belonging to the latter and acting within its bounds. However, here man introduces into the life of the world the principle of causality through freedom, i.e., creativeness. But this creativeness is not extramundane; it is cosmic and sophianic in its foundations; and at the same time it is partial, imperfect, weighed down by an admixture of the nonbeing out of which the world was created by God. Nevertheless, creativeness, as such, introduces something *new* into the world, which therefore cannot be understood as a finished mechanism: the world is actualized by man as well. But man does not create a new world; he only actualizes the created world, the world that is given and that, in conformity with this givenness, is capable of being actualized. The sophianic foundations of this creativeness are just as limitless as its attainments, for the world bears the image of the divine Sophia. Man is called to be the lord of

---

will', were a result of His human action, whereas the multiplication of the loaves of bread and the cleansing of the leper were a result of divine action." In general, "miracles are an act of God." "A result of the human action of the Lord was the fact that He took the maiden by the hand, whereas the return of her to life was the result of a divine action. These actions are different, even though in the God-Man's activity they are without separation from one another." "It is not the human nature that raises Lazarus; and it is not the divine power that sheds tears: tears are proper to the humanity, whereas life is proper to the hypostatic life." These Apollinarius-like statements are reinforced by a comparison (common also in Apollinarius) with the relation of soul and body. Of course, this comparison is applicable only to a human being who is composed of two elements, soul and body, but does not at all express the correlation of two wills and two natures in the one hypostasis of Christ. One gets a kind of alternation of the actions of the two natures, not their being without separation and without confusion.

the world, and to that extent the creator of it, in virtue of free creative causality in the world. The character of this free causality can be understood in terms of two relations: the relation of the human spirit to the natural world and the relation of the human spirit to the spiritual world. The human spirit is immersed in natural being; it is connected with the latter. This is a primary fact, which must serve as our point of departure. In itself this connection is a mystery of God's creation, in which is imprinted God's image, the life of hypostatic divinity in the divine Sophia. In human life this connection is disclosed in the history of man in the world. Man's spirit is united with the natural world through *soul*, which is the principle of human natural life.

This soul is distinguished from the animal soul by its conformity to spirit; it is *psuche noera*, the rational soul, in contradistinction to the "nonrational" animal soul. The hierarchical interrelation of these principles in man is such that the spirit has dominion over the soul, which manifests its life power in the natural world ("in the body"). However, in man, who is corrupted by original sin, this hierarchical interrelation has been violated in the sense that the spirit has fallen into dependence on the soul, and through the latter on the body as well: sensuous-animal being has acquired dominance over spiritual being, and the power of the spirit has been diminished accordingly. In his soul man bears all the laws of the cosmos, which now dominate him, but which he himself is called to dominate. The human spirit, insofar as it is in a normal hierarchical relation to the soul, has, through the latter, direct power in the world, and this without violating the world's natural laws, but rather fulfilling them. Such a normal hierarchical relation is absent in the fallen Adam, but it was realized in the New Adam, in the Lord Jesus Christ, who was truly perfect Man and therefore had power over the world in virtue of the obedience of nature to human freedom and to the purposes of the latter. But as we have seen, this gift of miracle-working also characterizes (although of course to a lesser degree) the righteous men of the Old Testament and Christian saints. Essentially, this very same dominance of man in relation to the world through the purposiveness of free causality also characterizes the "regulation of nature" which in general is realized by man; i.e., it includes the natural conquest of the world and the domination over matter. This is the gift of miracle-working disclosed in the integral life of humanity, in the life of the race. The difference between miracle-working and all the miracles of the regulation of nature in this respect is not a qualitative but rather a quantitative one. There where the miracle worker heals by word or by the direct command of spirit, medicine heals using means based on medical science. The *type* of relation of man to the world is miracle-working, i.e., the power of man over the world through free causality. Logos in man becomes the logos of the world.[4]

But the human spirit, in conformity with its essence, is defined not only in relation to natural being but also in relation to spiritual (albeit creaturely) being, and finally in relation to supramundane being, to the divine Spirit. Despite its incarnatedness and its connectedness with the natural world, the human spirit is not closed off from the spiritual world; on the contrary, it is always open for the action of the latter. As a creaturely spirit, i.e., as a spirit that is not absolute and not self-sufficient, the human spirit is always *inspired* from the spiritual world. Inspiration, emanating from one spiritual entity to another, is a manifestation of their being for each other and belongs to the very nature of spirit. Contra Leibniz, the windows of the spiritual monad are open. In other words, the creaturely spirit lives not only by its own nature, but also by the powers and inspirations of other spiritual entities; and the spiritual isolatedness of the creaturely spirit is ontological nonsense. The human spirit cannot remain empty; it does not belong exclusively to itself; rather, it is the intelligible *place of encounter* and struggle of dark and light powers, striving, each in its own way, to guide man in its direction. This does not at all mean that the human spirit itself is an *empty place* that seeks to be filled. No, it is an individually qualified spirit, having its own life and waging a spiritual struggle for its autonomous being; it chooses influences and is not just passively and powerlessly subordinate to them. Among these possible influences the first place belongs, of course, to divine inspiration, to that which the language of religion calls *grace.* Man is created in God's image and, as such, he is a receptacle of divine life and of the inspirations of the latter. Man,

---

4. This is the fundamental idea of my book *The Philosophy of Economy* (1911), an idea that I am now treating in a completely different aspect.

destined for deification in the fullness of his spiritual being, becomes a participant in the divine life without losing his own personal being. Such a maximally deified Man, in whom the entire fullness of divinity abided bodily, is the Lord Jesus Christ. As God, He had the divine life naturally; as Man, He was perfectly deified, so that between His divine and human natures, between His divine and human wills and energies, despite the *natural* difference between them, there was no separation or opposition in life, but rather they were united in the *one* life of the God-Man. Jesus was Christ, the Anointed, through the hypostatic descent and resting upon Him of the Holy Spirit in the Baptism; and this deification of His human nature He received by the feat of His life, by His suffering on the cross and death. The fullness of deification was manifested in the Resurrection, the Ascension, and the sitting at the right hand of the Father.[5]

---

5. It is in this sense that we understand the words of the apostle Peter in his discourse on the day of Pentecost: "Jesus of Nazareth, a man approved of God among you by miracles and wonders and signs, which *God did by him* in the midst of you, as ye yourselves also know: Him, being delivered by the determinate counsel and foreknowledge of God, ye have . . . slain. But God raised him up" (Acts 2:22-24; the King James Version has been modified). The italicized words do not have here a meaning that would nullify that which has been said about the human character of Christ's miracle-working. The whole context has in view only the idea of God's providential plan concerning human salvation. In particular, the words "God did by him [*epoiesen di autou*]" must be understood not in the sense that Jesus in His humanity was only an instrument of God's miracle-working power, but in the sense that the miracles were included in the disclosure and fulfillment of God's plan, just like the works of those who betrayed and killed Jesus. We find an analogous meaning in the apostle Peter's speech to Cornelius, in which the noted idea is expressed more clearly: "God anointed Jesus of Nazareth with the Holy Spirit and with power: who went about doing good, and healing all that were oppressed of the devil; for *God was with him*" (Acts 10:38). The idea that the miracles of the Lord Jesus Christ bore witness to the extraordinary grace of the Holy Spirit, abundantly resting upon Him, is also confirmed by the text in which the unforgivable sin of blasphemy against the Holy Spirit is mentioned. We find this text in all three Synoptic Gospels. It is most concisely, but most clearly, presented in Mark 3:21-30: "And when his friends heard of it, they went out to lay hold on him: for they said, He is beside himself. And the scribes which came down from Jerusalem said, He hath Beelzebub, and by the prince of the devils casteth he out devils. And when his friends heard of it, they went out to lay hold on him: for they said, He is beside himself. And he called them unto him, and said unto them in parables, How can Satan cast out Satan? . . . No man can enter into a strong man's house,

But grace as the active power of deification *changes* the human spirit. Grace makes the human spirit other than itself; it makes it stronger, more

---

and spoil his goods, except he will first bind the strong man; and then he will spoil his house. Verily I say unto you, All sins shall be forgiven unto the sons of men, and blasphemies wherewith soever they shall blaspheme: But he that shall blaspheme against the Holy Spirit hath never forgiveness, but is in danger of eternal damnation: Because they said, He hath an unclean spirit." This establishes a direct connection between the prohibition of blasphemy against the Holy Spirit and blasphemy against the works and miracles performed by the power of the Holy Spirit and attributed by the scribes to the unclean spirit. The narrative in the Gospel of Matthew of the one possessed with a devil, blind, and dumb, is similar (12:24-32): "But when the Pharisees heard it, they said, This fellow doth not cast out devils, but by Beelzebub the prince of the devils. And Jesus knew their thoughts, and said unto them, Every kingdom divided against itself is brought to desolation; and every city or house divided against itself shall not stand: And if Satan cast out Satan, he is divided against himself; how shall then his kingdom stand? And if I by Beelzebub cast out devils, by whom do your children cast them out? therefore they shall be your judges. But if I cast out devils by the Spirit of God, then the kingdom of God is come unto you. Or else how can one enter into a strong man's house, and spoil his goods, except he first bind the strong man? and then he will spoil his house. He that is not with me is against me; and he that gathereth not with me scattereth abroad. Wherefore I say unto you, All manner of sin and blasphemy shall be forgiven unto men: but the blasphemy against the Holy Ghost shall not be forgiven unto men. And whosoever speaketh a word against the Son of man, it shall be forgiven him: but whosoever speaketh against the Holy Ghost, it shall not be forgiven him, neither in this world, neither in the world to come." Here the visible power of the Holy Spirit is separated from and opposed to the Bearer of this power, the Charismatic: the word spoken — by ignorance — against the Man will be forgiven, but opposition to the overwhelming power of the Spirit of God is spiritual suicide, destroying the spiritual foundation of a man, and therefore it can be forgiven neither in this world nor in the world to come. But in the given case the power of the Holy Spirit is manifested and attested precisely in Christ's miracles, and therefore here He Himself views Himself as a Spirit-bearing Man. The text in the Gospel of Luke is the least clear. Here the Lord's saying that interests us is contained in a teaching about the leaven of the Pharisees, about divine Providence, about the confession of the Son of Man: "And whosoever shall speak a word against the Son of man, it shall be forgiven him: but unto him that blasphemeth against the Holy Spirit it shall not be forgiven. And when they bring you unto the synagogues, and unto magistrates, and powers, take ye no thought how or what thing ye shall answer, or what ye shall say: For the Holy Spirit shall teach you in the same hour what ye ought to say" (Luke 12:10-12). One can discover endless meanings in these texts on the blasphemy against the Holy Spirit, but it is clear that one thing they point to is the Spirit-bearingness of the Lord Jesus Christ.

powerful, more dominant in the world. The man upon whom grace is bestowed receives the power to become the natural god, the lord of the universe. His ability to be the logos of the world through spiritual causality, his liberation from slavery to the elements, increases together with his deification. And this power of the spirit, acquired by him not through the training of his natural powers (yogism, occultism) but through grace, is miracle-working in relation to the phenomena of natural life. Therefore, according to His gracious, deified humanity, the Lord was also the Miracle Worker; and He thus summons gracious, deified humankind to do works which He Himself did, not in the sense of repeating them, but in the sense of having in them a pattern and an ideal task. This is expressed in the commandment concerning works which Christ repeatedly gave to His disciples and which, in the Last Discourse, He made His testament, as it were (this is a text of supreme theological importance, which we have already cited several times): "Verily, verily, I say unto you, He that believeth on me, the works that I do shall he do also; and greater works than these shall he do; because I go unto my Father" (John 14:12). The words, "because I go unto my Father," signify, without doubt, the *fullness* of the accomplishment of the redemptive feat and of the power of the divine Incarnation: through the Passion to glory, through death to Resurrection and heavenly glorification, and through glorification "all power is given unto me in heaven and in earth" (Matt. 28:18). All this in relation to the world and man signifies the foundation of the Church as the Body of Christ, with Christ living in it, with the power given to Christ's humankind and with the "works" entrusted to the latter. This signifies Christ's inspiration in humankind, accomplished by the Holy Spirit. Christ's humankind in the world is called to become a cosmourge,[6] doing the works of Christ and manifesting His miracles. "Again I say unto you, That if two of you shall agree on earth as touching any thing that they shall ask, it shall be done for them of my Father which is in heaven. For where two or three are gathered together in my name, there am I in the midst of them"

6. The words "cosmourge" (i.e., performer of works in or upon the universe) and "cosmourgy" (i.e., working in or upon the universe) are formed by analogy with theurge (or demiurge) and theurgy. — Translator.

(Matt. 18:19-20).[7] The Church is the life of grace in which, first and foremost, man is saved from sin, receiving the remission of sins: thus, the Lord in His miracle-working combined the forgiveness of sins, spiritual healing, with bodily healing (cf., e.g., the healing of the man sick with the palsy [Mark 2:5-11]). But the Church is also the restoration of man in his strength. The path of man's salvation, the overcoming of the Old Adam in the New Adam, is the assimilation of the grace of salvation and life in this grace, i.e., in faith and in *works*. Here we approach the final, concluding question — the question of salvation in works: In what works? And in works or in a work? Do works have the significance solely of ascetic exercises for the soul, or do they also have a definite content?

Here one must have in view the personal path of every individual man in his spiritual destiny (for "the human soul is worth more than the whole world"), as well as the path of humankind as a whole, for an individual man is a member of humankind. The gracious inspiration of good in man gives him a spiritual power that is intrinsically absent in him: "the power of God is accomplished in infirmities." This power is manifested not only in the personal spiritual achievements of a given man, but also outside of him, in the whole natural and human world. Man is given the ability to surpass himself. He performs works in the world by virtue of spiritual causality; and this means that he works miracles, whatever they might consist in. And insofar as he acquires this power and inspiration from God's grace received in prayer, it is said that a man, through prayer by the power of God, can work miracles ("can move mountains"). Even more than this, every sincere prayer already works a miracle, i.e., it is an action of spiritual causality in the world, even if we do not see its outward manifestations. However, a man must not set miracle-working as an independent object of his achievements, for then he would become a magus, seek-

---

7. The fact that miracles are accessible to man is also attested by the Lord's words spoken to the disciples when they asked Him: "Why could not we cast him out? And Jesus said unto them, Because of your unbelief: for verily I say unto you, If ye have faith as a grain of mustard seed, ye shall say unto this mountain, Remove hence to yonder place; and it shall remove; and nothing shall be impossible unto you" (Matt. 17:19-20). This passage speaks at the same time of the power of faith and of the accessibility to this power of the works performed by the Lord.

ing signs.[8] In other words, there can exist a dark inspiration which can give the power to perform false signs, just as there can exist the greatest spiritual power which, however, does not manifest itself outwardly as direct spiritual causality in the world: John the Baptist did not work miracles (John 10:41); nor did the Mother of God in the course of her earthly path (at least within the bounds of the Gospel history). In any case, the seeking of signs is an attribute of little faith and is condemned by the Lord. However, it is insufficient to pose the question of miracle-working solely in connection with the destinies of individual men, because the relation of man to the world is not only personal but also communal in character; it is also accomplished in the historical process. This relation to the world, the conquest of the world through spiritual causality and purposiveness, is the calling of humankind, constituting the necessary condition of the very existence of the latter. In relation to the world humankind is a multi-personal cosmourge, a "master," conquering nature and subordinating it to its own, human purposiveness. This relation is implanted in man, and it must be understood religiously. And first of all it is incorrect to separate and oppose the two paths of causality — personal miracle-working and the cosmourgic conquest of nature. On the other hand neither path violates the bounds of natural possibilities; both paths are naturally lawful. And one can even say that one and the same action, e.g., the healing of a sick man, can be a work both of personal miracle-working and of medical science; furthermore, in one epoch and in one environment a particular work might be considered an example of miracle-working, whereas in another epoch and environment it would be an ordinary natural act (e.g., vision and hearing over a distance). Miracle-working and cosmourgy belong to the same domain — man's spiritual causality in nature. In this sense one should not oppose them or prefer one to the other, because each of them is given its own place and time.[9]

8. Cf. the narrative of Acts 8:9-11 about Simon Magus, who "used sorcery, and bewitched the people of Samaria, giving out that himself was some great one: To whom they all gave heed, from the least to the greatest, saying, This man is the great power of God. And to him they had regard, because that of long time he had bewitched them with sorceries."

9. One saintly lover of God once said (Rufinus being his source) that the desert-dwellers of the Thebaid used to cross the Nile on crocodiles and had no need of boats. If we

But human cosmourgy is subject to spiritual self-determination, for it can mean different things: It can be miracle-working in the Name of Christ, in fulfillment of His commandment; and it can be a further submergence into the world, with spiritual enslavement by its elements and service of the lust of the flesh and of the eyes; and finally it can become a false miracle-working, with false signs and directed against God. Cosmourgy is also proper to natural man as connected with the world; and therefore, although there takes place in it the disclosure of the powers of natural man in nature, nature's humanization and spiritualization, cosmourgy inevitably acquires different attributes depending on the type of human inspiration that is involved. The character of the human inspiration can differ; there can be three kinds of inspiration here: first, humankind can be a cosmourge, like the Church, in the name of Christ, performing works of love and philanthropy, and then cosmourgy becomes a Christian miracle-working, not personal, but communal, ecclesial; and then the ecclesialization of the world occurs through cosmourgy. Secondly, humankind can make its cosmourgic power into an instrument that serves its natural essence damaged by sin, i.e., into an instrument that serves passions and the void. On this pathway and in this domain significant possibilities of the humanization of the world and of natural miracle-working can be achieved, although, spiritually, this miracle-working remains void and sinful. Thirdly and finally, cosmourgy can also become a pathway of theomachy, a satanical antagonism toward God and an exhibition of signs of *human* power, where man considers himself to be god. And since, when it has awakened to a certain degree, the human spirit cannot remain neutral, this power becomes the throne of "the kingdom of the beast," i.e., of theomachy.

---

keep in mind only the comparison of these two modes of transportation — crocodiles and boats — each is of course good in its own time; however, in our time it would be not only strange but even sinful to attempt to cross rivers on crocodiles, and the desert-dwellers of our time would of course use only boats for this purpose. This example shows the whole *relativity* of miracle in its outward manifestation. Spiritual causality through cosmourgy therefore naturally eclipses sporadic, individual spiritual causality through miracle-working or, in any case, changes the domain of this latter causality, and in our day the domain of physical miracles has naturally been curtailed in favor of moral or spiritual miracles.

All three modes of man's relation to the world struggle but coexist in the cosmourgic process. The spiritual struggle that is tearing the world apart, the spiritual tragedy of the world that constitutes the content of history, is disclosed here too, in human cosmourgy. Cosmourgy also belongs to the church, as does all of human life. Natural cosmourgy must be made into a Christian miracle-working, by subordinating it to the spirit of Christ. That is what the Gospel miracles mean for us; that is what they speak about and what they summon us to: They summon us to an active relation to the world, to cosmourgy, in the Name of God. "If ye shall ask any thing [of the Father] in my name, I will do it" (John 14:14). The salvation was preached by the Lord with "God . . . bearing . . . witness, both with signs and wonders, and with divers miracles, and gifts of the Holy Spirit, according to his own will. For not unto the angels hath he put in subjection the world to come" (Heb. 2:4-5; the King James Version has been modified), but to man. "For in that he put all in subjection under him, he left nothing that is not put under him. But now we see not yet all things put under him" (2:8).

We can stop here. The Gospel miracles represent individual works of compassion, responses to human sorrow and need, "healings and good works." And for the entire human cosmourgic path they give a pattern of good works in the name of merciful love. And this is more than sufficient for the sanctification and understanding of human work.

IV

On the Resurrection of Christ

Miracles are *works of God* which are given to man. However, there arises here the following, and final, question: Can these scattered works be related to some *one common work,* which includes everything and to which everything is subordinated? Does the Lord not indicate to us this common work, which, as such, surpasses by its commonality all separate works, when He says: "He that believeth on me, the works that I do shall he do also; and greater works than these shall he do" (John 14:12)? What is greater than that which is done by Him? Here, the distinction is not quantitative, of course, but qualitative. This distinction is therefore connected with that event which, in itself, contains the foundation for these "greater works." This is the *Resurrection of Christ.* One must not forget that He accomplished His "works" in the days of His earthly ministry, prior to the Resurrection, after which He will go to the Father (John 14:12) and acquire from God all power in heaven and on earth; and He enables His Church too to participate in this power or, rather, in the service of it. What is the *Resurrection* of Christ viewed as a miraculous act *among* Christ's miracles? Is it *one* of the miracles, albeit the greatest one; or is it separate from them, instead constituting Miracle in the proper, unique, ontological sense? Yes, the Resurrection of Christ is an ontological miracle that *takes us beyond* the limits of this world, even though it is accomplished in the latter; it is super-cosmic in the cosmos. In order to better understand its nature, let us first see what the New Testament says about it. Here we find multiple testimonies about Christ's resurrection, first of all as a fact: Christ is risen, risen from the dead (Matt. 28:6; Luke 24:34; Rom. 8:34; 1 Cor. 15:54). The texts of this character do not contain an explanation of the fact itself, and sometimes only the practical applications of it are given (1 Cor. 15; Rom. 6; etc.).

Further, the words of the Lord Himself contain a repeated anticipation of His sufferings and resurrection: "From that time forth began Jesus to shew unto his disciples, how that he must go unto Jerusalem, and suffer many things of the elders and chief priests and scribes, and be killed, and be raised again the third day" (Matt. 16:21; cf. Mark 8:31; Luke 9:22; 24:7; Matt. 17:9; Mark 9:9; Matt. 17:22-23; 20:18-19; Mark 10:34; Luke 18:33). In all these texts the sufferings, the death on the cross, and the Resurrection are viewed as a single act in which the sufferings are the path to the Resurrection, and the latter is the culmination and task of the entire earthly work of the Savior (but the disciples did not understand these words: "And they kept that saying with themselves, questioning one with another what the rising from the dead should mean" [Mark 9:10]). The Resurrection is the final goal of the Lord's coming to the earth. How was it accomplished? Was it a work accomplished by Christ's command, like His other miracles: "see, be cleansed, rise and walk, be cast out," etc., or was it accomplished in another manner than they, not by Christ Himself or, at least, not directly by Him? In the New Testament we have a whole series of texts that have one and the same content, express one and the same idea: The Resurrection of Christ was accomplished in such a way that "God hath raised up [*anestesen*] Jesus of Nazareth, having loosed the pains of death: because it was not possible that he should be held by it" (Acts 2:24, 32; the King James Version has been modified). This was spoken by the apostle Peter in his first discourse at Pentecost; and he repeated this in the discourse on the healing of the lame man: "God hath raised [Jesus] from the dead, *ho Theos egeiren ek nekron*" (3:15); "God . . . raised up his Son Jesus" (3:26). The same thing is repeated in the discourse of the apostles Peter and Paul before the high priests (4:10), in Peter's discourse in the Sanhedrin (5:30), in Peter's discourse to Cornelius (10:40), and in Paul's discourses in Antioch (13:30, 32, 37) and in Athens (17:31). In other words, we find this feature repeatedly in the apostolic preaching. This idea is expressed repeatedly by the apostle

Paul in his epistles (Rom. 4:24; Rom. 10:9; Col. 2:12; 2 Cor. 4:14; Gal. 1:1; Eph. 1:20; 2:5-6; 1 Thess. 1:10; cf. 1 Peter 1:21). In particular, we find the following idea in the apostle Paul: "But if the Spirit of him that raised up Jesus from the dead dwell in you, he that raised up Christ from the dead shall also quicken your mortal bodies by his Spirit that dwelleth in you" (Rom. 8:11); also: "Christ was raised up, *egerthe*, from the dead by the glory of the Father, *dia tes doxes tou Patros*" (6:4). Also applicable here is the text Hebrews 5:7, where salvation from death (i.e., through resurrection) is represented as the work of the Father in answer to the Son's prayer: "in the days of his flesh . . . he had offered up prayers and supplications with strong crying and tears unto him that was able to save him from death, and was heard in that he had reverence" (the King James Version has been modified). Indirectly applicable here is also the text John 5:26: "as the Father hath life in himself; so hath he given to the Son to have life in himself."

The general idea expressed in these texts consists in the fact that Christ's resurrection took place through His raising by the Father, by His will and glory (divinity), and that Christ was raised by the life-giving Spirit. How should one understand this idea in relation to the two natures of Christ and His two wills and energies? How is their interrelation defined in Christ's fundamental work, in His Resurrection?[1] What in the Resurrection can be seen as a work of the human nature, which could work other miracles by human power; and could this human power in Christ perform its own resurrection, while remaining within the limits of humanity? That is the ultimate question in the theological understanding of the Resurrection in connection with the general doctrine of miracle.

Here our thought must ascend to the foundations of the divine Incarnation, according to which Christ assumed true humanity, with the exclusion of sin. His human nature was the same as that of the original Adam, with all of its possibilities but also with all of its limitations. Nevertheless, Christ's human nature differed from the nature of the original Adam, in-

---

1. This question must confound those theologians who view all of Christ's miracles solely as a manifestation of Christ's divine power through man, i.e., as a *deus ex machina*. By the same token these theologians would be naturally compelled to extend this idea to the resurrection of Christ as well, and to see in the latter His own miracle performed on Himself, whereas this is directly contrary to Holy Scripture.

sofar as Christ's nature bore the necessary consequences of Adam's Fall, which retained their power despite Christ's total sinlessness, these consequences including hunger, thirst, fatigue, and so on; and therefore the sinless flesh assumed by Christ from fallen and weakened humanity was different in state from what Adam's flesh was before the Fall. However, this difference did not change the essence of the matter, because it did not erase the image of God in fallen man. What were the possibilities and the limits for Adam's human nature, particularly in relation to death? Man was created perfect, but this perfection even in Adam was not a final and definitive one. Spirituality of the flesh was given to him only as a natural harmony by virtue of God's creative act, but this spirituality was not assimilated by him. Man still faced the task of conquering — by his freedom through spiritual causality — his flesh, of spiritualizing the latter; and it was for that purpose that there was given to him God's commandment, which showed what he still had to acquire through freedom. Although he was not created mortal (as Catholic theology teaches), the original man was not immortal either. Death as a possibility (*posse mori et non mori*[2]) was contained in his bodily nature, not yet spiritualized by man himself; and this possibility became a reality as soon as the spiritual equilibrium in him was disrupted by the power of sin. If Adam had not fallen, he would have continued to live for an indeterminate period of time without being subject to death, but also without having the power of immortality, which is not contained in the human essence itself. (Of course, we cannot know the ways of God on which the positive victory over death would have been accomplished in Adam.) It was this sinless flesh of Adam — potentially mortal although not subject to death — that was assumed by the Lord. Natural death was not proper to the flesh assumed by the Lord, just as it was not proper to the flesh of Adam, but the possibility of death was contained in both of them. But such a death could only be a violent one: Christ could only "be killed," precisely in virtue of His true humanity. This death, like every *human* death, was just as natural as it was unnatural, in consequence of the fact that all that exists is created for life, and that God did not create death. As an unnatural and, so to speak, ontologically nega-

---

2. The possibility of dying and not dying. — Translator.

tive act, for every living being death is the sickness of sicknesses and the suffering of sufferings, which break the ontological bonds of the living being, the bonds uniting soul and body. The spirit is immortal and does not die, but "shall return unto God who gave it" (Eccles. 12:7). (That is why the Lord cries out on the cross: "Father, into thy hands I commend my spirit" [Luke 23:46].) Death separates the soul, quickened by the spirit and quickening the body, from the body, which becomes a corpse and dust; and this loss of the soul's bodily attachment to the world, this transformation of energy into potential, in virtue of which a man is transformed from an incarnate being into a fleshless spirit (which is unnatural for him), introduces an inner rupture into human life. It is very important to establish precisely *where* this separation occurs. It occurs not between the spirit on the one hand and the rational soul and body on the other (that would signify disincarnation, i.e., not only death but annihilation of the human being), but between soul and body, with the connection between spirit and soul being preserved in the afterlife world. Such a trichotomic conception of death is expressed in the church hymn: "in the grave in the flesh, in hell with the soul as God," etc.[3] Based on this discussion, we can approach two questions: What was the death of Christ in His divine-human essence? And, in connection with this, what was His Resurrection?

It is perfectly evident, first of all, that death, like suffering, does not affect His divine essence, which in its eternal life abides above time. Christ's divinity in the God-Man creatively contains and providentially permits these events without interacting with them and, in general, remains above the temporal process. One can say that God in the God-Man was not born, did not suffer, did not taste death, did not rise from the dead, and did not ascend to heaven, for He always abides in imperturbable eternity. But the hypostasis of the Logos as a human hypostasis becomes a subject of human life in all its fullness and, thus, of human death with all its power and all the horror of contact with the nonbeing out of which man was called to life by God's creative act. And one can even say that the death of Christ was the most horrible of all deaths, for it was violent and unnatural: It was not at all necessary for the sinless man to die. If a sinful man starts

---

3. From the Paschal Hours troparion. — Translator.

dying on the day of his birth (for sicknesses are the beginning of death), the New Adam, the sinless man, did not know sicknesses and had nothing to do with this constant inner death, ceaselessly anticipated, to a certain degree, prior to its actual advent. He knew the state of human "growth," up to the advent of perfect maturity, but without the reverse process of decline. The power of life and the ontological love of life were therefore greater in Him than in all other men. And therefore He could experience the approach of death only spiritually: "My soul is exceeding sorrowful, even unto death" (Matt. 26:38). And the agony of Gethsemane is not only the redemptive sorrow of compassionate love concerning human sins; it is also the resistance of the living human being to death, a spiritual agony: "O my Father, if it be possible, let this cup pass from me: nevertheless not as I will, but as thou wilt" (26:39). And we also see this in the divine-forsakenness on the cross, which is a dying, a sense of submergence into nonbeing. This represents the real gates of death, beyond which a new life beyond the grave is revealed, but which are unavoidable and constitute, properly speaking, the horror of death: "And about the ninth hour Jesus cried with a loud voice, saying, Eli, Eli, lama sabachthani? that is to say, My God, my God, why hast thou forsaken me? . . . Jesus, when he had cried again with a loud voice, yielded up the ghost" (Matt. 27:46, 50). Without doubt, we have here a terrifying picture of genuine human dying with its horror, and with extreme intensity. Perhaps someone will say that not all deaths are so painful, and that there are peaceful deaths without agony, without horror (although we do not have the knowledge to judge what happens at the threshold of death). To this the answer must be that there never was and could never be a human death deeper (so to speak) and more terrifying, more unnatural, than the death of Jesus, this death from undiminished fullness of life. In this death, creaturely *possibility* is actualized, but there is no *necessity*: From the point of view of Jesus' human nature, it did not have to be. "Therefore doth my Father love me, because I lay down my life, that I might take it again. . . . This commandment have I received of my Father" (John 10:17-18). However, the fact that this death was voluntary, in fulfillment of the Father's will, does not abolish its unnaturalness or its reality. Christ's assumption of genuine humanity, i.e., of the *creaturely* nature that arose out of nonbeing and ontologically participates in the latter in death, is nowhere so manifested in its truth as in His death; but, conversely, in-humanization *without* the acceptance of death would have been decorative, docetic. On the contrary, one can say that, in His life, Christ encountered Death in all its power, which did not stop at swallowing up even this perfect man, but one who nevertheless was creaturely in His humanity. Death manifested its power over His creatureliness; and if, in His humanity, the New Adam contained the whole of the human nature, His death too was an all-human death, the death of the whole Adam, both Old and New (see Heb. 2:14-15).[4] The genuineness of this death is by no means contradicted by the fact that it was a voluntary sacrifice, pre-eternally accepted in God's council and in accordance with His human freedom. Death extends its shadow over His earthly life before it actually arrives. The Lord knew in His divine-humanity (i.e., on the basis of His divine omniscience as well as on the basis of His human, prophetic prescience) that death was awaiting Him, and about this He warned His disciples as well as all the people, telling them repeatedly about the sign of the prophet Jonah and about His own three-day sojourn in "the heart of the earth" (Matt. 12:40), as well as about the three-day destruction and restoration of the Temple (John 2:19-22) (which was used against Him as testimony by false witnesses at His trial). But the fact that the Lord foresaw His death does not in any way abolish its reality and power, just as His sufferings did not become less genuine from the fact that He had foreknowledge of them. Thus, the Lord's death, of course not according to His divine nature but according to His human nature, was a *genuine human death,* consisting in the separation of soul and body, and this was the death of His humanity, the subject or spirit of which was the Logos Himself: in this capacity of His as *human hypostasis,* God Himself died in man by the human death of the human nature. The fullness of death is also manifested in the fact that it lasted for three days: this was not a swoon, but a real separation of soul and body, during which the soul had its life in the world beyond the

4. "Forasmuch then as the children are partakers of flesh and blood, he also himself likewise took part of the same; that through death he might destroy him that had the power of death, that is, the devil; And deliver them who through fear of death were all their lifetime subject to bondage." Cf. Hebrews 10:5-10.

grave, and descended into hell to preach to the dead. In these three days (*in triduo*) there is some sort of mysterious meaning of the *fullness* of death, of the ripening of it, only beyond which does the Resurrection arrive. During these three days the Savior's body was as dead as that of any human deceased, although it did not become a corpse, i.e., it was not subject to corruption (Acts 2:31; 13:37; Ps. 16:10). This does not lessen the fullness of death, which consists in the separation of soul and body, and which did in fact occur here.

Although it is united with the body through the intermediary of the soul, the human spirit in this life acquires a certain direct connection with its body, a connection that can be preserved even after death: Even though this is not life, it represents a certain imprint of the spirit in the dust of the earth. This anticipation of resurrection is, so to speak, the potential of resurrection, although, by itself, it is powerless to realize the latter. This connection, which does not lend itself to further understanding, makes it so that, for every man, death is nonetheless not a disincarnation. Even though, in their actual state, spirits of the dead who retain a memory of their bodies are similar to bodiless spirits, they nevertheless differ from the latter precisely by this connection, as a potential of incarnation realized in the future resurrection; while in relation to the flesh this potential is expressed in a certain spiritualization of matter. What we get is a paradoxical relation: Death destroys the connection between *soul* and body, i.e., it terminates the activity of the principle that quickens the body, but it does not abolish a certain connection between *spirit* and body, although this connection is not the life of the body. The spirit lives in the body only through the soul, the connection with which the spirit does not dissever even after death, although there is now no possibility to realize life. The spirit of the deceased, being inseparably united with the soul, also preserves a connection with the body. In this sense although the body of every man after his death is in its corpse state already not a body, it nevertheless is a *relic* (as the Trebnik[5] calls it). A relic is a former body which, having become a corpse, decomposes, returning its matter to the natural elements, but which, in some part of itself (a grain, a primary atom), pre-

5. "The Book of Needs," a collection of Orthodox prayers and rites. — Translator.

serves its connection with the spirit; and the reality of this connection is the greater, the greater was the power of the spirit over the body in life. Therefore, in holy relics, this connection with the body of the deceased is felt with great immediacy, which is the basis of their veneration.[6]

During the three-day sojourn in the grave the Lord's body too was in the state of a holy relic; in general, it was the archetype of holy relics. The connection of the body with the divine spirit, a connection acquired by the power of this spirit over the body and soul in the Savior's earthly life, became so indissoluble that Christ's body, even though it was dead inasmuch as the soul had departed from it, did not become a corpse, i.e., it did not "see corruption"; and in this sense (but only in this sense) it was not dead, but found itself, as it were, in the state of a deep swoon, in a state of "sleep" (cf. the verse from the church hymn: "He fell asleep in His flesh as if dead"). This incorruptibility of the Savior's body results from the power of the divine Spirit living in it, as well as from the special character of the death of the New Adam, which, being unnatural for Him as a consequence of His sinlessness, was coercive and violent, and thus could not be as effective as for all other men in the sense of destroying the connections between spirit and body. However, it is only this incorruptibility of Christ's body that distinguishes Christ's death from all other human deaths. It was for this reason that, in the grave, Christ's body was hidden from the face of the earth, like the bodies of all dead men.

Let us now return to the fundamental question: What was the Resurrection of Christ in relation to His two natures? For the prevailing point of view this question does not even exist: in the patristic literature (even in the scholastic systematizer John of Damascus) there is no special examination of this question, and the above-indicated twofold character of the texts concerning the resurrection is left unnoticed. It is accepted without any particular discussion that Christ rose by His own divine power, so that "the Resurrection is a document of the true God" (to quote Vladimir Solovyov). But such a view is of course a de facto Monophysitism, where the participation of the human nature is reduced to pure passivity, i.e., is

6. See my essay "On Holy Relics." [This essay is presented as the first part of the present volume. — Translator.]

simply absent. And on the other hand such a simplified understanding of the matter directly contradicts the texts where it is said that the Father raised Jesus by His (the Father's) Spirit, i.e., where Christ's resurrection is depicted not as an act of Jesus, not even one that is accomplished by His divine nature, but as an act of the Father and, together with Him, of the Holy Trinity — an act that, in a certain sense, is accomplished *upon* Jesus. The two sides of the question are organically connected. Let us begin with the first.

We have examined Christ's miracles as acts of His human nature, deified and anointed by the Spirit, within the limits and laws of this world, although they represented an extension of the boundaries previously accessible to man. Can these boundaries be extended even further, in order to give a place to the *human* victory over death, which victory would be not just a temporary raising of the dead, who will again be swallowed up by death, but the achievement of a new and immortal life?

Evidently, *they cannot be*. Death is not something episodic in life, something that can be overcome (like a sickness). It is the dark foundation of life: Life, having been called out of nonbeing and therefore deprived of absolute stability, in essence became *mortal life;* and this is not an episodic state but the fundamental quality of life. It is impossible to overcome this quality from within, for this is the *metaphysical* boundary of life. What is needed is an ontological change in the very quality of creation, which the latter cannot perform upon itself; that is to say, what is needed is a new creative act performed *upon* creation, a new act of the Creator that would return the fallen creature to its original state and, even more than that, would give it a higher degree of spirituality, which was absent even in the original state. This transition from *posse non mori* to *non posse mori*[7] can only be a new creative act of the Creator performed upon creation, an act that now presupposes not only God's providential activity in the world which sustains, preserves, and guides the latter within its own limits, but also His creative activity, which takes the world *beyond* these limits.

Thus, what we have here is the Creator's act of wisdom and omnipotence, which are revealed in the *creation* of the world. However, there is also

---

7. From the "possibility of not dying" to the "impossibility of dying." — Translator.

a substantial difference here. God creates the world out of nonbeing by His command, and the nothing hears this command and obediently carries it out — the world arises. In this first creation all the activity belongs to the Creator, whereas creation is characterized by a total passivity proper to nonbeing, which in itself does not have anything and is only a metaphysical place or, according to Plato, a receptacle *(ekmageion)* of creatures. But in the new, or *second*, creation, which is what resurrection is, instead of the void of nonbeing we have the created world and man in it. The Lord does not abolish His first creation; instead, He gives it the power of His eternity, He gives it stable being. In the new act of creation the Creator now creates not out of nothing; instead, He *re-creates*, forming the new creature out of the old, interacting with the old creature without destroying it, i.e., without doing ontological violence to it, but rather metaphysically elevating it.

The first act of the new creation is the Incarnation, the Annunciation, and the Birth of Christ: The Father sends the Son to be born of the Virgin by the Holy Spirit, with the Virgin saying from the person of creation, "Behold the handmaid of the Lord; be it unto me according to thy word" (Luke 1:38), and the Annunciation and Birth of Christ are accomplished. In relation to the world the Birth of Christ is a new creative act of God, surpassing the world; and in this sense it is an absolute miracle. And the second absolute miracle, the culminating miracle, similar to and connected with the first, is the Resurrection of Christ, which also is a creative act of God in the world and which, as such, is accomplished by the entire Holy Trinity. The Lord's Resurrection was accomplished by divine power; all are agreed about that. However, usually this refers to the action of the divine nature in Christ, in virtue of which Christ Himself raises Himself from the dead, i.e., rises from the dead but is not raised. However, according to the witness of Holy Scripture, He does not rise by Himself, but is raised by the Father through the Holy Spirit. This means that the Resurrection was the work of the entire Holy Trinity, just like the creation of the world: the Father commands by the Son and accomplishes by the Holy Spirit. This is precisely the action of the Holy Trinity. This does not mean, consequently, that, in the Resurrection, the Son only fulfilled the Father's will but did not participate in it Himself. The inner hypostatic life of the Holy Trinity is thus disclosed: the beginning, the will, belongs to the Father; the fulfill-ment belongs to the Son; the accomplishment belongs to the Holy Spirit ("for the Father loveth the Son, and sheweth him all things that himself doeth" [John 5:20]). As "one of the Holy Trinity," the Son too raises Him-self, but He does this in the capacity of God the Creator, not in the capacity of the hypostasis of the human nature by the power of the latter. In the Resurrection of Christ, divine power is communicated to man by a new creative act, which is expressed in the Resurrection of Christ. Therefore, the future resurrection of all of humankind, preaccomplished in Christ, is actualized now not by a special creative act of the Father and, together with Him, of the Holy Trinity (although it is spoken of with application to man too; cf. 1 Cor. 6:14; 2 Cor. 4:14; Rom. 8:4) but by Christ in His provi-dential activity: "For as the Father raiseth up the dead, and quickeneth them; even so the Son quickeneth whom he will. . . . the dead shall hear the voice of the Son of God: and they that hear shall live. For as the Father hath life in himself; so hath he given to the Son to have life in himself" (John 5:21, 25-26). "I will raise him up at the last day" (John 6:40). "For as in Adam all die, even so in Christ shall all be made alive. But every man in his own order: Christ the firstfruits; afterward they that are Christ's at his coming" (1 Cor. 15:22-23).

The new creative act of the Holy Trinity, which the raising from the dead is, presupposes (in contrast to the creation of the world out of noth-ing) a certain interaction between Creator and creation. What is the par-ticipation of creation in this interaction? According to the testimony of the apostle Peter, "God hath raised [Him] up, having loosed the pains of death: because it was not possible that He should be held by it" (Acts 2:24; the King James Version has been modified). Why is that so? This necessity of Christ's Resurrection according to His humanity, what does it consist in? Death turned out to be possible for the God-Man not because it had sufficient grounds for itself in His personal being, the way it has power in relation to the Old Adam and, in him, in relation to every individual hu-man person. On the contrary, according to His personal sinlessness, He had to be free of death, at least in the same way as the original Adam be-fore the Fall. But since He had received the nature of the Old Adam, which was weakened by sin and had become mortal, together with the infirmity of this nature He had also received death (Phil. 2:7-8). Thus, the death of Christ contained this contradiction: It was a manifestation of the life of the *race* as opposed to the life of the *Person*, and this alone was the reason why "it was not possible that He should be held by death." The personal principle battles with the generic principle and overcomes it. In the life of Christ's holy soul there was nothing that could weaken its power over the body and its life-giving force. His holy soul was *worthy* of immortality, for it was obedient to the divine Spirit who had given it life. The Lord followed His entire earthly path in complete obedience to the Father's will, and His human will and activity agreed fully with this will, although this agreement was not so natural and painless as in the case of the original Adam before the Fall; rather, it was burdened by all the infirmity of the damaged human nature. It was necessary to tame and to bend this will even unto a sweat of blood: "not as I will, but as thou wilt" (Matt. 26:39). And if in the course of His entire earthly path to Golgotha He could say about Himself, "My meat is to do the will of him that sent me, and to finish his work" (John 4:34), the end and culmination of this path was voluntary acceptance of the Passion and of death, of which He was not worthy, for they did not correspond to His sinless nature. Nevertheless, in obedience to the Father's will, He remained to the end in inviolable acceptance of Adam's nature and without any desire to transcend, remove, or lessen the burden of this nature by Divine power ("Thinkest thou that I cannot now pray to my Father, and he shall presently give me more than twelve legions of angels? But how then shall the scriptures be fulfilled, that thus it must be?" [Matt. 25:53-54]). And there was no limit to this obedience except death, which completed and exhausted the obedience. In this obedience to the Father's will, which also became the Son's own human will, Christ manifested total lordship of spirit over soul and body, thereby actualizing the inner norm according to which Adam was created. Through the spirit Christ mastered the flesh; and He had to become a spiritual, immortal man. However, the assumption by Him of Adam's nature condemned Him to death even *despite* His personal victory over the flesh. Christ shared death with the whole human race, and this was the last tribute to the genuineness of the Incarnation. And this death was more terrifying and painful than that of every other man, for here bonds of life were being torn apart that were not internally damaged by anything. Just as the bodily sufferings and wounds of the most pure body caused torments that were incomparably greater than any other human torments, and just as the moral torments caused by human sin and malice were, for the sinless perfect holiness, more terrifying than for all other men, so Christ's death was the most excruciating and terrifying death of all the deaths ever experienced by men.

Nevertheless, just as the power of immortality no longer existed in Adam's essence, *by nature* it did not exist in Christ's human essence either. On the cross the connection between soul and body was torn apart by death, and Christ's soul remained connected with the Logos without a body. His soul was worthy of having this power of immortality because of its holiness, because of its conformity with the divine Spirit, especially since from the beginning man was endowed with immortality if he would not lose it, for "God did not create death" (Wisd. 1:13; translated directly from the Russian Bible). Christ *deserved* the victory over death because of His feat, for "in the days of his flesh . . . he had offered up prayers and supplications with strong crying and tears unto him that was able to save him from death, and was heard in that he had reverence" (Heb. 5:7; the King James Version has been modified); and He could pray about Himself: "I have glorified thee on the earth: I have finished the work which thou gavest me to do. And now, O Father, glorify thou me" (John 17:4-5). And Christ's soul *receives this power of resurrection from God:* God raises Christ and Christ rises by the power of His soul over the body — the raising is also the Resurrection. This communication of the power of immortality to the human soul, received into the hypostatic union of the Logos, is God's creative act performed upon the human nature: This nature is *deified* by the communication to it of the power of immortality in the body. It is also the *glorification* of the human nature: "Now is the Son of man glorified" (John 13:31).

Bodiless spirits are immortal by their nature, in virtue of the simplicity and noncomplexity of their ontological structure. They do not die, for there is nothing in them that dies; and they do not have the possibility of dying, even when spiritual dying takes place in them, and angels become demons. Man could become mortal precisely as a consequence of the complexity of his ontological structure and the instability of his ontological equilibrium, for in this structure the spirit is united through the soul with the body, through which it is united with the whole world. And the power of immortality in man in this sense is different from that of the angels, because it comes not from the absence of flesh but from the mastery and spiritualization of flesh. Therefore, the raised body is the spiritual body. This is not a new flesh or a new world, but a renewed, transfigured, spiritualized one, changed not in its substance but in its state. Christ's human essence was deified through the hypostatic union with the Logos, "for in him dwelleth all the fullness of the Godhead bodily" (Col. 2:9). With respect to the *hypostatic union* of the divine and human natures in Christ there is, of course, no difference in the degree of deification: One and the same Logos was the hypostasis of Christ in His birth, in His baptism, and in His death. But the same thing cannot be said about the degree of the deification of the human *nature* in the sense of the ability to receive the power of this deification. It is natural for a human being to live in time, to grow and to develop. Therefore, our Lord too, as Man, passed through different ages, to which corresponded different degrees of *fullness* in the unfolding of the human nature, different degrees of deification: Among such distinct watersheds one can enumerate the Baptism, then perhaps the Transfiguration, and then perhaps the glorification prior to the Passion (at the arrival of the Greeks, John 12:20-33). It is remarkable that the approach of each of these watersheds is accompanied by the action of the entire Holy Trinity: by the word of the Father and the visible (or invisible) action of the Holy Spirit.

The Resurrection is also such a watershed, but one that in its significance surpasses all the others. This act would not have taken place if man had not been prepared to receive it in his human maturity and his creaturely freedom. But when the human nature in Christ reached its maximal maturity, when it was perfected and became worthy of this gift, to it was given the fullness of divine life in deification. Christ's human nature received the power of resurrection. His soul, spiritualized by the Logos, received the power to retrieve its body: "his soul was not left in hell, neither his flesh did see corruption" (Acts 2:31; cf. Ps. 16:10). In this body death is defeated, and divine fullness has totally abolished the nonbeing out of which the body was formed. This is a new glorified body. And although the Lord worked miracles in the course of His earthly ministry, only now does He bear witness to the culmination — after the Resurrection: "All power is given unto me in heaven and in earth" (Matt. 28:18; cf. what the apostle Peter says in his discourse: "God hath made that same Jesus, whom ye have crucified, both Lord and Christ" [Acts 2:36]). The Resurrection of Christ, accomplished by the power of God in the human being worthy and capable of receiving it, can be juxtaposed with the Annunciation and is, as it were, the new act in the Incarnation itself, the culmination of the latter, for the human being becomes completely transparent for divine life. And if man is created in order to be a god by grace, then the perfect Man in Christ is God by the unshakeable unity of His human life with the divine life. The temporality of His human existence is abolished in the fullness of deification, and the *aeviternitas* of humanity is identified with the *aeternitas* of divinity, in the unity of creaturely and noncreaturely eternity. This fullness of deification of the human nature in Christ, which is also the glorification of this nature, is indicated in Christ's high-priestly prayer as the supreme goal of the Incarnation: "Father, the hour is come; glorify thy Son, that thy Son also may glorify thee: As thou hast given him power over all flesh. . . . And now, O Father, glorify thou me with thine own self with the glory which I had with thee before the world was" (John 17:1-2, 5).

The Lord abided in the grave for three days; and this three-day sojourn, so insistently foretold by the Lord Himself, is the holy term of fullness, for His mysterious abiding with His soul in hell as well as for His Resurrection. These three days were the time when His human soul, being separated from the body but preserving hypostatic unity with the Logos, received the power of resurrection. These three days, shut off from us by an impenetrable veil of mystery, are a certain substantial portion of time in the salvific Incarnation. We can glimpse in the fullness of this time interval a certain ripening of the soul toward the reception by it of the power of resurrection, which should be understood not as an external act, a *deus ex machina*, but as a creative disclosure of the original powers of the human nature under the life-giving rays of the seeing of God by the soul liberated from the body as yet untransfigured by resurrection. And like all that is human, this culminating act presupposes for itself a definite term; it takes place in time, which does not end for the God-Man with His death on the cross. This time does not end for Him even after the Resurrection, although Christ's humanity enters here into new conditions of existence in the resurrected glorified body. This is the beginning of a new completion of the term, of a new time: the mysterious forty days during which the Lord abides in His Resurrection, if not on earth, then above the earth, if not with His disciples and in general not with men, then nevertheless appearing to them. He Himself bears witness to Mary Magdalene about the significance of these days: "I am not yet ascended to my Father," but "I ascend unto my Father, and your Father" (John 20:17). And only after the completion of this forty-day ascent does the Ascension take place, i.e., only after this completion does *time end* for Christ's humanity and is His life submerged in the life of the Holy Trinity. However, the final time of completion, already in heaven, occurs only after the Ascension: This is the ten-day period before Pentecost, after which Christ, "having prayed the Father" (see John 14:16), sends from Him the Holy Spirit upon the disciples. After this, time in Christ's humanity completely dissolves in eternity, merges into it. However, for us, for His earthly humankind, time remains, and times and seasons also remain. Christ rose from the dead and, in Christ, rose all of humankind, which, however, still lives by the mortal life of the Old Adam. Between the resurrected glorified humanity of Christ and our humanity there exists an ontological discontinuity *(transcensus)*, which cannot be filled by any movement from one to the other. But, at the same time, there remains an inner connection or even an indissoluble unity between the Son of Man and the human race, according to the promise: "I am with you always, even unto the end of the world" (Matt. 28:20), in conformity with His abiding on earth in the course of forty days after the Resurrection, in conformity with His presence in the Eucharistic body and blood, as well as in His abiding in the world in the blood and water that poured out of His side.[8] Christ lives both in the individual man

---

8. See our essays "The Holy Grail" (1932) and "The Eucharistic Dogma" (1930). [Both available in B. Jakim's English translation in *The Holy Grail and the Eucharist* (Lindisfarne Books, 1997). — Translator.]

(Gal. 2:20) and in His humankind, acting in them and giving them new powers. And in the Last Discourse Christ leaves His humankind, the Church, in the persons of His disciples, the following testament and promise. Referring His own works to the Father, He summons us to believe in the Father on the basis of His works: "Whatsoever ye shall ask [of the Father] in my name, that will I do, that the Father may be glorified in the Son" (John 14:14). "The Comforter, which is the Holy Spirit, whom the Father will send in my name, he shall teach you all things, and bring all things to your remembrance, whatsoever I have said unto you" (14:26; the King James Version has been slightly modified). "The Spirit of truth . . . will guide you into all truth: for he shall not speak of himself; but whatsoever he shall hear, that shall he speak: and he will shew you things to come" (16:13). "And now I have told you before it come to pass, that, when it is come to pass, ye might believe" (14:29). The Last Discourse not only contains great promises but summons us to great works, whose pattern was given by the Savior: "If I had not done among them the works which none other man did, they had not had sin" (15:24).

And so, is the earthly life of humankind with its works connected with the coming resurrection of humankind, which has already been accomplished in the Resurrection of Christ? We cannot affirm that there is a direct connection, for there is a *transcensus* here, an absolute miracle, God's new creative act; but we cannot rule out such a connection either, for what will rise from the dead is not a new humankind, but the very same earthly humankind. However, our thought cannot grasp this connection, for there is a miracle here, a miracle that tears apart our thought with its law of logical and natural continuity. Resurrection cannot enter our consciousness as a goal, as one of the goals, even if the final one; nor can be it eliminated from our consciousness as a guiding idea, as an ideal of reason (Kant). Resurrection cannot be attained and actualized by human powers alone within the limits of the earthly world with its causality, a world that is also destined to be transfigured, to become a new heaven and a new earth, for God who raised Christ transfigures and raises from the dead — Christ raises us from the dead (see John 5:20-30).

But does this nullify the connection between the life of this age and the Resurrection? Can the Resurrection be understood only as a one-sided act of God, a divine act of salvific coercion performed upon the creature, in virtue of a kind of divine arbitrariness, without any interaction with the creature? Was the very coming of Christ not accomplished in the fullness of the times and the seasons? Did this coming not presuppose for itself a series of human accomplishments and achievements in all humankind and in the Old Testament Church? And on the other hand does the history of the Church exist only in order to prepare for the coming of the Antichrist with all manner of corruption and disbelief, and in general is the result of this history reducible, not just to a pure zero of good, but even to a minus? Of course not. Even if this result is the final separation, it is also the final accomplishment. And if that is the case, then all the human *works* to which Christ summons us and of which He gives the pattern in His miracles, all these works *have a relation to the end,* i.e., to the Resurrection; from the human side, all of them lead to it. This does not eliminate the action of the Father's omnipotence upon the world, but it is also not an ontological coercion of the creature. Therefore, just as works have their integral in the Work, so miracles have their integral in the Miracle. It is impossible for us to define their relationship more precisely, not only because divine culminating action is inaccessible to man, but also because here it is a question also of *man's creative tasks,* with the participation of freedom and inspiration. That which man should do, but can fail to do, cannot be known in advance, for it is something new in history. Here, prevision and prophecy fail, and only the testament of creativeness, and the supreme goal of the latter, speak to us. Man cannot know in advance what humankind will attain or not attain on its path. Moreover, different possibilities exist here, and therefore prophecy is only conditional. The only thing we know is what man's goal is. The works of humankind serve life, which is God's abiding miracle in this world; and thus these works must lead this temporary life to the life of the Resurrection, which is God's Work performed upon human works. The universal resurrection is therefore the divinely actualized integral of all of human history and all human works. This is what is said about the heavenly Jerusalem: "And the nations of them which are saved shall walk in the light of it: and the kings of the earth do bring their glory and honour into it. . . . And they shall bring the glory and honour of the nations into it" (Rev. 21:24, 26).

Index